"Art is a human activity consisting in this, that one man consciously by means of certain external signs, hands on to others feelings he has lived through and that others are infected by these feelings and also experience them"

Count Leo Tolstoy
"What is art?" 1898

The Hawthorn Scent

Of an Irish Springtime and a spiritual journey

- An autobiography in verse -

Derick Bingham

THE HAWTHORN SCENT
© Copyright 2000 Derick Bingham

Front cover and illustrations by Ross Wilson

ROSS WILSON is an artist and sculptor.
He is well known for his fascinating C. S. Lewis Centenary Sculpture 'The
Searcher' placed in East Belfast. His work can be found in places as diverse as
the James Joyce Museum, Dublin, The National Portrait Gallery, London and
Harvard University, Cambridge, USA.
He lives with his wife, Liz, in Portstewart, Co. Londonderry.

ISBN 1 84030 093 0

Ambassador Publications
a division of
Ambassador Productions Ltd.
Providence House
Ardenlee Street,
Belfast,
BT6 8QJ
Northern Ireland
www.ambassador-productions.com

Emerald House
427 Wade Hampton Blvd.
Greenville
SC 29609, USA
www.emeraldhouse.com

To five significant influences on my poetry

To: Grace Payne, philanthropist and Christian
stateswoman who unlocked it.

To: Sophia Hillman King, Assistant Director of the Institute
of Irish Studies at The Queen's University of Belfast who
further helped me to see that it was worth unlocking.

To: Medbh McGuckian, poet, who has been
Writer–in–Residence at the Queen's University of Belfast and
Visiting Fellow at the University of California, Berkley who
encouragingly set out vital markers for it's journey.

To: Angela Fee, schoolteacher and homemaker who underlined
the importance of its being accessible.

To: Geoffrey Ballie, gifted accountant with a sharp eye for
punctuation who helped give it cadence.

In this unique autobiography-in-verse the author traces his journey from childhood by the beautiful Mountains of Mourne through his school and University days to adult life. He writes of the challenge of a call to the Christian ministry worldwide and of serving through years of terrorism and civil strife. Here is a kaleidoscope of people who have crossed the author's path and experiences that have shaped his life. It is an autobiography that is wistful, sometimes exhilarating, sometimes sad, often humorous but always filled with hope.

By way of introduction

Life is filled with touches. The sweetness of a long kiss backed by fidelity. The power of a story well told. The searing wound of sarcasm. The bewildering influence of a cold shoulder. The enlightenment of a good teacher. The fickleness of hype. The sound of the cataracts of death around the bend. The clutch of a little baby's hand on an adult's small finger. The shadows cast by moonlight. The greeting of the rising sun. The sound of rain driving against a bedroom window. The inspiration of a great orchestra. We are all touched by something.

Professor Brer of "Little Women" fame told Jo to write about what she knew and one evening at the Linenhall Library in Belfast Dr. Higginson of Victoria College looked me straight in the eye and she said ,"You know that you know". Here then are some of the things that have touched my life on my spiritual journey. I trust that what is good will touch you, too. It all began in an Irish Springtime.

Derick Bingham
Autumn 2000

"I'll never go back", in her heart she said,
As the hawthorn blossom its glory displayed.

Of Aughlisnafin and the
hawthorn scent

My first memories are of Aughlisnafin,
Of drumlins green and yellow whin,
Of running water and furrows deep,
And candlelight and pillowed sleep.
A long road ran to McEllroy's,
A general store that held no toys,
But bags of seed and well cured ham,
And the many needs of a farming man.
Farming wives would buy there, too
Though a war had made their choices few.
On the counter stood the final word
On all the purchases that occurred.
It was a set of scales that weighed all out
And gave the attendant his commercial clout.
On Lucozade bottles my memory rests.
I ripped their yellow cellophane wrappings with zest;
Only bought, though, when real sickness came,
But enviously glanced at just the same.

I loved to climb the hill to that store,
Though only a child approaching four.
Living on the farm of my mother's birth,
Midst childhood's tears and fears and mirth,
While our new home was built from my parents' dream
Where Slieve Donard's breast rose by golfing green.
In May, Spring brought life to that countryside ~
It cascaded bluebells far and wide;
Stickleback followed the rush of the stream
And many whirlygig bettles were seen.
The hay crop started to thicken up
And the lemonade man left us soft drinks to sup.
Back from Africa, swallows swooped into the barn
And a scent began wafting around the farm:
From hawthorn blossom on tree and hedge
Touching me too by that long hill's edge.
In my family's history the hawthorn scent
Brought a turning point after my mother went
Purposely up that hill past that store
Because from life she wanted a whole lot more.
She had boarded a liner from Southampton dock
And had joined the busy immigrant flock.
At nineteen she certainly had been very brave
To leave Aughlisnafin via ocean wave,
And in Boston, Massachusetts she first cast her lot
And started a little doughnut shop.
Eight years later she came down that hill;
"A wee run home" had been her only will.
When she smelt the scent from the hawthorn there,
Any North American dream, no matter how fair,
Died in her heart at that very moment
As she walked down from that long hill's summit.
"I'll never go back", in her heart she said,
As the hawthorn blossom its glory displayed.

Interestingly, over three hundred years before,
A ship sailed from the Netherlands' shore.
More passengers joined her at Southampton
And eventually from Plymouth, she crossed the Atlantic Ocean,
Making land in Massachusetts at a spot near to Cape Cod;
And the Pilgrim Fathers did not think it odd
That when their ship had been built she was happily named
"The Mayflower", now in legend famed.
The mayflower, of course, is the hawthorn blossom
And I think it really is quite awesome
That the flower linked with emigration brought my mother back ~
An intruiging coincidence in History's track.
A return ticket for the liner "Queen Mary", of course,
Lay in my mother's pocket, but, the source
Of her decision to stay lay deep in her heart
And from that decision she would never depart.
For, truth is, if pixies on your own doorstep are not on hand,
You'll certainly never find Fairyland.

And so to bed, up the narrow stair
Holding a candle making shadows, there,
All along the little bedroom wall.

Of the wee blue blossom
and some champ

To Claragh school I went on many a day
And on the humpback bridge I used to play;
Beneath its hump, beside the stream
Of many an exploit I would dream.
By the flax dam, too, I would pass an hour,
And a symbol it was of historic power:
For in 1871 I am reliably told
Ulster's linen was internationally sold
From 68 mills and over 40,000 folk
Of the wee blue blossom gladly spoke.
The Huguenot refugees hugely mastered techniques
Of spinning, weaving and bleaching those sheets
Of linen cloth then made into lace
Or sails, or towels or pillow case.
The Quakers from England developed the trade
And the Richardson family name was made.

I was underage for school but was permitted
To accompany my brother Desmond and was admitted
To a desk at Claragh school with the other pupils
And with that I certainly had no scruples.
I enjoyed the fun we had in the schoolyard
And my first days at Academia were far from hard!
Memories now flood my mind of sunlit days
When I mounted a tractor completely unphased
And sat on the mudguard like a king
And as the plough dug in my heart would sing
To see the rich, dark brown earth unravel
As across the field we slowly travelled.
Birds avidly followed my Uncle Wesley and I
Swooping on worms with ecstatic cries;
And that grey Ferguson tractor with rasping gear
Had a sound that brought those birds no fear.
Harry Ferguson, of course, was a man amongst men,
And on August the eighth in 1910
He flew Ireland's first plane from the County Down shore ~
As my mother watched with thousands more.
They called him the "Mad mechanic from Dromara town",
Henry Ford's only partner, now renowned
By his portrait on Ulster's bank notes that circulate
As buying and selling meet their fate.
The newly turned sod we left behind.
Darkness fell and down came the blinds.
The lamp wicks were lit and the log fire crackled
And the day's pressures were slowly unshackled.
My Aunt Lily's food was *par excellence* ~
Ulster's cuisine she certainly advanced.
She made her own butter out of the churn,
To golden yellow it quickly turned.
I loved to see her with wooden blades slap
The butter into shape, to soon fill that gap
Between toast and jam or to fill the lake
In champ which many children make.

Champ is mashed potato creamed with milk and butter
With added chopped spring onions and in Ulster
It is a favourite dish and with a spoon
A child can make a champ lake, soon!
And so to bed, up the narrow stair
Holding a candle making shadows, there,
All along the little bedroom wall.
And then, the land of Nod would call
With dreams warmed up by a hot water bottle
As childhood's gentle sleep would settle
And the sound of cawing rooks receded
As I the Sandman's lulling heeded.

Above the entrance door sat a lion of stone ~
He kept a sharp eye on us, up there, alone.

Of Ballywillwill and a marbled hall

Often we left that farm on the hill
And went to the little hall at Ballywillwill.
There we met light from hissing gas
And heat from a pot-bellied stove would pass;
And the ticking clock on the wall would measure
The hours I spent there with boyish pleasure.
For I loved that wee place of humble stance,
As my Bible knowledge slowly advanced.
We sang of Heavenly sunshine, side by side,
And of a cleansing fountain deep and wide,
And of a woman who went searching down by the door,
Under the carpet and all over the floor,
And of the wise man who built his house upon the rock ~
Then to the "tea meeting" we children would flock.
In the dead of winter that hall seemed to heave,
As plump women and gangling men would seize
Sandwiches, buns and steaming cups of tea ~
There was no collection, it was all free.
A gifted speaker would tell of the Gospel, pure;
And of a Saviour whose love was forever sure.
Then came the time to get a prize,
And attendance records brought hearty surprise.

Some had an unbroken record with full reward
(A long clap the crowd would them afford)
And others would a consolation prize receive
As they sat upon their mothers' knees.
Zipped Bibles were received by many a child
And picture framed texts by boys who ran wild.
A gleaming red apple to all was given,
And soon through the frost or snow we were driven.
On our short journey gentle moonlight was shed
As we made our sleepy progress to bed.
Of Wrights, McNeills and Hagans we talked
And Watsons and Nixons, all Protestant stock.
Around us the Roman Catholic neighbours looked on
With benevolent eye, till we were gone,
For no violent words were ever breathed around
From that tiny platform in County Down.
It was Christ who was preached and lifted high
As those post war families struggled by.
Ballywillwill House enthralled my youth
Built in 1815 it was not uncouth.
That memorable house was our Mansfield Park
And in our lives it made its mark.
It was our Blenheim Palace and our Northfield Hall,
Its outstanding features I can still recall.
Its Classical pillars stood high and firm
And there a seminal truth I learned.
Above the entrance door sat a lion of stone ~
He kept a sharp eye on us, up there, alone.
And large parties of folk would gather inside
As guests of Sam Wright and his kindly bride.
In the huge sitting room we sat in a circle of seats
Till the magic call came "It's time to eat";
And high-heeled shoes I can still hear click
In the marbled hall which interlinked
The sitting room and dining room, fine
Where the magic call had bid us dine.

To a child what is spacious looks incredibly huge
And that spread table my young eyes bemused.
It seemed somewhat like the coming heavenly feast
Or a mighty earthly banquet, at least.
Bond Walker's large canvasses hung on the wall ~
And the artist was often there, erect and tall,
Speaking gentle, kindly words of note
Watching carefully every word he spoke.
For he was a Godly man who shunned all hype
A Saint, I'd call him, true to type.
Then came the time when we would all retire
To the sitting room and gather around the fire.
I recall one occasion when Mrs Wright
By the piano sat down towards the end of the night.
She played and sang some words of a song
Which haunt me still though fifty years have gone.
A song it was of the love of God
Its vast reach and depth it did applaud:
It said if the ocean were made of ink,
And of this my mind began to think;
It added that if every blade on earth were a quill,
And this suggestion gave me a thrill;
It then imagined every man a scribe
And this scene my little mind imbibed;
And to top it all it then boldly said
What if the sky were of parchment made?
Then Mrs. Wright's voice quietly sang out
What those metaphors in song were all about:
That to write God's love on such a sky
Would drain that ocean completely dry,
And that parchment would never, ever contain
All you could write in such a vein.
Later I learned that the words had been found
On an asylum wall but had not been drowned
In the confines of that immediate place
But surfaced to quickly move apace,

And are now found in hymnbooks across the world
As history around their truth has swirled.
Then Nina the maid came to take me to bed.
Up the cantilevered staircase I was led
And in a bedroom warm and snug I slept
While the adults their adult fellowship kept.
Then I was taken by my mother after midnight's hour
To be wrapped in a rug and put into the car.
In the back seat I was gently laid
And dark telegraph poles past my window sped,
And as on my back I sleepily lay,
I inspected the illustrious Milky Way.

There the conquerors of Everest were we,
Fangio or even Custer at Wounded Knee;

Of the Queen of watering places
and the valley of the Braid

The new house was finished on the Bryansford Road
And my parents just loved their new abode.
Newcastle: "The Queen of watering places,"
My father would say to the upturned faces,
For he was an Evangelist of gentle demeanour ~
A truly much beloved figure.
All over Ulster he would constantly travel
And the Gospel story he would unravel.
He sometimes got discouraged in his Godly work,
And her duty my mother never shirked
To encourage him to go on preaching God's truth ~
And they said he preached the Gospel according to Ruth!
County Antrim was his special place.
To villages like Broughshane and Buckna he would set his pace;
And for a Sunday "Breaking of bread" service he was seldom late,
Travelling across country in his Morris Eight.
Many hundreds of folk came to Ballymena Town Hall
As with the gifted David Craig he preached to one and all
And a harvest for God over years was made
All along the valley of the Braid.

And the God who led Patrick, associated with Slemish Mountain,
Helped my father draw from His spiritual fountain.
No Elmer Gantry was Fred Bingham
And thousands of people truly loved him.
The world I lived in through those childhood days
Was based in a town of quiet ways ~
Of Edwardian hotels and the Donard demesne
Where the Glen River flowed from abundant rain,
On whose rocks we played on many a day
And to Donard Lodge we found our way.
Ruined by fire it was but a hulk
But of its present self we did not sulk.
For we called it "The Castle", and to us it was
The centre of many a daring cause.
There the conquerors of Everest were we,
Fangio or even Custer at Wounded Knee;
Jim Hardy of Wells Fargo was a hero then,
And the Famous Five and the Secret Seven.
With my friend Willie Hagan I spent many an hour
Playing at "The Castle" gripped by imagination's power ~
Willie went on to become an airline pilot
But in those days he was a "Castle" zealot!
In wartime, American officers had often dined there
And in Victorian days many a lady, fair.
The Annseley family had owned the Lodge and the demesne
And my mother sent me, now and again
To the Annseley Estate office, down by the sea,
To pay for our water which did not come free.
In that large demesne there was a door in a wall
Which led to a house, which stood quite tall.
The McRoberts lived there and to my brother and I
They showed much kindness, and I do not lie
When I say that Lily McRoberts would truly be
One of the kindest people I would ever see;
She was tall and beautiful and somehow to me

Her gentleness was unforgettable: I played in its lee.
Why she showed me such patience I'll never know
As to that home I would frequently go.
Children are often a pain in the daily round
But if loved then that love will come around,
To become a memory that is not sad,
And my memory says "She made my childhood glad."

"Wo-beak", cried Frankie and his horse would stop
And into his cart he would lift me up;

Of crying "Wo-Beak"
and a good doctor

An era was passing, though I knew it not.
John Alexander's forge, with its iron red-hot,
Was fun to stand in of an afternoon
But its time was receding. Though very soon
In its confines a unique new "guider" was made
Its ball bearing wheels put others in the shade.
Desmond and I now had the best "guider" in town
And from many a hilltop we hurtled down!
In Doctor Gibson's driveway, though, I brushed death's gate
When I crashed into his wife's grey Standard Eight.
In the Doctor's home and garden we often played
And Grandpa Gibson's honey was handsomely spread
On many a sandwich on summer days
As we restlessly pursued our childhood's ways.
Muriel Gibson mothered us with her Southern brogue
And took "The Irish Times", (in our home not in vogue);
And was so patient with us through her crowded life
Of a very accomplished doctor's wife.
And I recall that many a childhood dream
Was dreamt with a reversing car not seen
But heard as the Doctor went out on call
As illness or death in our town touched all.

A finely skilled yachtsman was "Doctor Jim";
Through childhood fevers we listened to him;
Talk of his adventures far out at sea
And from a scourge he later tried to set me free.
He emphasised the importance of stepping out of the daily grind,
And of what I now call Brer Rabbit's "Laughin' place" to find.
My father's greatest problem the Doctor could trace
To his inability to relax from the daily pace.
So depression gripped his gentle psyche
And broke his heart, though, it seemed so unlikely
That such a public figure could actually know
Depression's wild and dark undertow.
Another local personality in my memory stays
He was a carter through Newcastle's labyrinthine ways.
"Wo-beak", cried Frankie and his horse would stop
And into his cart he would lift me up;
And the world then looked a very different place
To a little boy with a grinning face.
Frankie held his arm straight up to greet
Those folk he passed upon the street.
"How are ye?" he would cheerfully say
As his horse Dolly sauntered on her way.
He lived at "Eagle Cottage" on Shan Slieve Drive
And he made us glad we were alive.
I reckon many adults can still hear
The words "Wo-beak" sounding in their memories' ear.
He need not have stopped but he always did,
And Frank Connelly's kindness made its bid
To stay in hearts long after he was gone
As part of our childhood's innocent song.

"What time is it, Mr Wolf?", we'd holler
As on the wolf would steal each scholar.
"It's ten o'clock", the wolf would cry

Of a wolf and grief

St. John's Primary was my local school
And its headmaster certainly was no fool;
For with pipe and brain Mr Garston led the way
To knowledge for pupils day after day.
My first teacher was Miss "Cluckey" McClure ~
Why we called her Cluckey I am not sure.
She built learning with each carefully laid brick
But she did it with the aid of a hazel stick.
Of all the occasions I cannot forget
Was the day she flailed Ina who would not let
A tear flow as she came by my place
With embarrassment and pain all over her face.
Oh! Ina Polland I don't know where you are
But time after time in my life so far
I've thought of that day Cluckey hurt you so sore ~
I can still see your eyes as you crossed that floor.

Of course Cluckey made us all learn how to knit,
Which in a boy's life did not seem to fit.
"In through the bunny hole and round the big tree
Out through the bunny hole and pop goes she"
Was the rhyme that was often repeated,
As we knitters at our desks were seated!
In the schoolyard we often played a game
And its question was always the very same
"What time is it, Mr Wolf?", we'd holler
As on the wolf would steal each scholar.
"It's ten o'clock", the wolf would cry
And we with much relief would sigh;
And take a step closer hoping we wouldn't get caught
When he'd cry "Dinner Time" and our lives would be sought!
Somehow pain and misery seem to wrap the time
I spent in that little school of mine;
Of shutting a door on Jane Mills' finger
And on its healing time I will not linger;
Although at the time she would have thought it absurd
That she would one day arrange my flights round the world.
There was one bright place, though, in my life
And a journey there certainly brought no strife ~
To Percy Ogle's shop we were bound by an umbilical cord
And there spent what money we could afford.
It was called "The Fountain" and it certainly showered
My nose with sherbet and my taste buds fired,
And squibs we would buy with childish glee,
And from blue touch paper we would flee,
And in the mouth Rowntree's pastels disappeared much quicker
Than Rowntree's wine gums which were very much thinner!
And Eddie Whiteside helped Percy in her white coat
From our daily round they were not remote.
They were kind and Percy always smiled
As his "sweetie" counter my thoughts bequiled.
I also loved "Greenaways", the town's little toy shop,

And I liked Archie Cairns, its owner, a lot.
Toys in their box wrapped with brown paper and string
A lot of pleasure to my childhood would bring.
Maybe that's why to this present time,
I prefer a boxed present from any friend of mine!
The most memorable holiday of my life as a lad
Was a trip to London that I had.
Mr. Tom Tughan took me with him on a business trip
And of the great sights of the city he gave me a sip
And I love London to this very day
Because I was introduced to it in such a kindly way.
I sadly found, though, that the playground wolf
Had a real counterpart who was not aloof,
For he brought sin into the world, the Bible says
And death by sin which came one day
And wrapped on our door when I was seven
And my father's soul went home to Heaven.
I remember gazing on his body cold ~
Its frightening silence a story told
Of the last great enemy we all face
Whose devastating work is not hard to trace.
"His place will be missed", the death column said
As across the country newspapers spread
The news of his passing to village and town,
And deep sorrow was felt by many around
The Province where his preaching had touched many a heart,
And in whose spiritual history he played a part.
Dozens of people came and stood in our garden
As farewell hymns surrounded his parting,
And hundreds made their way out to Drumee
Where the final service I can still see.
Hawthorn Baillie's Churchillian voice rose in prayer
As Desmond and I stood silently there;
Of its solemn tone I can still hear the sound
And our father's body was laid in the ground,

And the gravedigger's spade, as heartless as ever
Poured the thudding soil to immediately sever
All sight of a father wise, gentle and true,
Whose sincerity thousands of people knew;
And we filed out of that cemetery on Drumee hill
And the night closed in, silent and still.

The man who taught me was a hero in war
And his life had always held the scar
Of losing his captain in a blazing plane
While he was ordered out and very quickly gained
Momentum and parachuted free
And landed upside down in a tree.

Of my captain and a meeting with Browning

The nineteen fifties were gathering pace
When my mother a decision now had to face.
She did for me what I'll never forget,
For she took me out of my Primary School set
And she sent me each day to Downpatrick town
To a new school on which I did not frown;
For though its premises were once the County Gaol
The pleasure it brought me would never fail
To fill my life with deep gratitude
For the way it changed my attitude
To what a school can actually do,
To mould a life with visions new.
The school stood in a town where history's paths meet;
There was Irish and Scotch and English Street;
The Courthouse stood there and the Commercial Hotel
And in the town the hangman's noose often fell
On many prisoners across the years,
As they stood awaiting death with overwhelming fears.
St. Patrick is believed to have been buried in the town,
And there many Georgian doorways can be found.

At the start of my new schooling I didn't do well at all
And it took time for me to heed Wisdom's call;
To pursue knowledge and all the treasure it holds
And to relish the secrets it always unfolds.
I failed the dreaded "Eleven Plus", twice
And I was capable of even failing it thrice!
Then at thirteen my life began to turn around
And I slowly began to make new ground.
Maths was my weak point and my brain
Tried to get around theorems, all in vain.
"Bingham's lost in the long grass," the headmaster would say,
And around that long grass I would often flay,
Until I suddenly got a longing to pursue
A dream which was completely new.
I decided that to University I would like to go
And its many challenges I wanted to know.
Arthur Fowweather, or "The boss" as we nicknamed him,
Had an office which was near to the gym
Of Down High School and on his door I knocked,
And in his room, pungent with tobacco smell, my desire I unlocked.
I think he nearly fell off his seat
For my exam results showed near academic defeat.
"If you'll work I'll help you", he generously said
And that day my scholastic fortune was made ;
For after school he coached me week after week
As my thick brain began to seek
Pythagoras and company's clear solutions
To Geometry's many convolutions.
"You should thank the Lord every night," he stated
"For Pythagoras" and to that I surely related
As the square on the hypotenuse was truly equal
To the sum of the squares on the two sides in sequel.
At last my Junior Examination I passed,
And of fees my mother was free at last,
And I entered a world which opened up

As from knowledge's fountain I began to sup.
How can I ever describe, though, the hour
When a new horizon opened with gentle power?
The sun was streaming through the windows and still
Down Cathedral stood silent sentinel;
And beyond the school wall stood the "Mound of Down" ~
It was there even before the Normans came around.
Believed to be the ancient palace site
Of the Kings of Ulster in their own right.
And with those historical icons surrounding me,
I was sitting in an English class where, so deftly,
Mr. Watts was expounding words before my sight
From Robert Browning's poem entitled "Meeting at Night."
It was the story of a lover's boat gaining a beach
And two hearts beating, each to each.
The man who taught me was a hero in war
And his life had always held the scar
Of losing his captain in a blazing plane
While he was ordered out and very quickly gained
Momentum and parachuted free
And landed upside down in a tree.
Then he walked the length of occupied France,
Leading the enemy a timely dance,
Pretending he was a Polish peasant ~
A journey that was dangerous and far from pleasant.
Norrie Watts was not, though, a man of war,
For one day I asked him in a school corridor
What he thought of Churchill who had just died,
Who so powerfully the enemy had defied.
The nation was paying Churchill its last respects,
Believing he'd been its saviour elect.
"We don't want another Churchill", he gently said
As to the staff room his way he made.
It was not that he didn't honour Churchill, no:
It was that he hoped we'd never have to go

And fight in another such vicious war
The scars of which his generation bore.
He did not believe the old lie, did Norrie:
"Dulce et decorum est pro patria mori".
Ah! Captain, my Captain will you ever know
What you did for me as you gently showed
Browning's gift that day at Down High?
For Literature's key you did not deny.
And it unlocked a truly enthralling power,
Which has been my friend ever since, my teacher's dower;
And I wondered, as at my desk I sat,
If a heart would ever beat against mine like that?
And it did, while at school and others after,
With many a kiss mixed with tears and laughter,
Until one day a heart settled down,
And stayed beating against mine, my desire to crown.

Religious Instruction came from "Holy Joe" ~
Was there anything that man did not know?
The Rev. Thompson smoked like a chimney and ate like a king

Of Annie, Mamie
and Holy Joe

Characters were everywhere in that sprawling school,
Teaching our minds until they were full
Of French and Faraday and Fowweather, too
For his famous quips were right on cue.
"Bob's your uncle", he would firmly declare
And his brilliance just did not seem fair.
"Q.E.D" meant "Quite Easily Done"
For a problem I certainly didn't find fun.
"You might as well join the noble order of the Reccabites", said he
"As ever try to join A to B".
"Cunningham ,vous bletherez beaucoup de Barnamagherese",
He said with surprising verbal ease!
Though William Cunningham later got an outstanding degree
In the difficult discipline of moral philosophy;
He became a much beloved pastor
And of painting he is quite a master.
And Annie Rainsford had a squinted eye
And no matter how her students might try
To get away from her glance was not easy ~
It often made one feel quite queasy.

A more decent soul never walked our school hill
Than Annie, whose French is with us still.
Of pluperfect tenses she knew the meaning;
Which was more than the man who broke through the ceiling
As he worked above that little classroom
Trying to solve some paltry problem.
We all fell apart with hilarious laughter
And he lived much happier ever after.
Religious Instuction came from "Holy Joe" ~
Was there anything that man did not know?
The Rev. Thompson smoked like a chimney and ate like a king
His cloak covered his corpulence like a curtained thing.
"When I was in Nicosia", he would often say
As he wandered back to some chaplaincy day.
I can't remember a lot of what he said to me
Except that he often mentioned the Code of Hamurabee!
Now History was in another leaque:
Mamie Minnis my young mind intigued
With the story of a war where millions would die
Before the Treaty of Versailles;
Of Wilson, Clemanceau and Lloyd George
Who in the Hall of Mirrors a peace treaty forged,
The roots of which led to another war
Which cost the lives of millions more ;
Of Napoleon we learned and Cromwell too ;
The Queen of Scots and the valiant few
Who rode up the fearsome valley of death
Against Crimean guns with incredible faith.
Mamie wore lipstick so very thick
That I could hear her lips part, and she was quick
To encourage my mind History's map to trace
At an extremely absorbing and interesting pace.
I heard some joke with her about a "Killinchy muffler"
Was it something to keep out the cold of winter?
Ah! Time showed that she was deeply in love

With another History teacher, hand and glove!
He was called Noel Orr and at Advanced Level
His teaching gave balanced thinking amid Ulster's trouble.
The English were not perfect in Ireland, he would show,
Which amid fanatics was always helpful to know.
No biased teaching ever passed my mind
From his view of History, I would find.
He was a very thought provoking teacher to know
And my respect for him would constantly grow.
Tragic it was when terrorists killed his brother
And it was so sad to see his family horrendously suffer.
Mr. Cook or "Cookie" taught us Geography in depth
Of the Mediterranean and the Continental Shelf.
He stopped his schedule, though, one memorable day,
And taught us in an entirely different way:
For Kennedy and Khrushchev were facing it out
Over missiles in Cuba and both had clout,
And through every day of that nuclear crisis
"Cookie" kept us focused in his classes.
He was scared and so were we,
For an apocalypse we could plainly see
Hovered over our twentieth-century life
Until the Russians backed down from threatened strife.
But Geography was suddenly more than a subject
It was a living thing in which we were the object.

That those "Workers" our cards would deliver
In the manner and style of Long John Silver!

Of a red and white banner
and the Tipperary Wood

My childhood had passed and as I look back
What distinctives marked its busy track?
What lingers in my memory now?
As the years have gone, I would allow
That a red and white banner truly stands out
As a guide to what my life has been about.
It read C.S.S.M. and it gently was
A child's hand-maid for the Christian cause;
Called the Childrens' Special Service Mission
To intriguing days it gave free admission.
How very fortunate we as children were
For two weeks of each year to be in its care.
Each morning as the sea lapped in at "The Rock"
We would sit by the dozen and never mock
The beautiful truths of Scripture we learned
From Mr. Rankin and his team, deeply concerned
That foundations of faith in our lives be laid,
As Roxie Simpson's harmonium swayed;
Joyously wheezing out hymn and chorus
As the Irish Sea stretched out before us.

Mr. Rankin was a headmaster from Birkenhead,
Who was often in a striped blazer arrayed,
And he led his team, firmly, but with great cheer
As Christian truth he tried to make clear.
The "Birthday Service" was each year's highlight:
We looked forward to it with unbridled delight
Especially as to how the Birthday cards were brought
To that eleven o'clock service down at "The Rock".
One year a boat load of pirates rowed up
With knives in their mouths and would not shut up,
And with raucous interruption we all received
A Birthday card, and no-one was peeved
That those "Workers" our cards would deliver
In the manner and style of Long John Silver!
One year, if my memory serves me right
We all got a truly tingling fright
When the Fire Brigade in a Dennison truck,
With siren blazing, roared right up
To our Birthday Service and men poured out
To pass on Bithday cards round and about!
We wore red badges and the "Workers" wore blue
And every year a game we'd play anew.
It was called "Hunt the worker" and all around Newcastle
Those blue-badged workers gave us a lot of hassle
As they hid in many an intiguing diguise
And often, to our very great surprise,
We'd find them in the rarest places,
With twinkling eyes and solemn faces.
Behind all the fun was serious intent,
As to "Cissim" House or service we went.
One evening at a "Sausage sizzle" on the beach
The Saviour of the world my heart would reach;
There young people told of trusting Christ as Saviour
And how he had radically changed their behaviour,
· And later sitting on a sand dune beyond the Slieve Donard Hotel

I came to place my trust in that Saviour as well.
In Christ I received joy, grace and pardon
Helped to faith by Dr. James Barton.
What other childhood markers line memories lane
As my years now more than half a century gain?
There was beauty everywhere I could look
Beauty in many a "Crannie" and "Nook",
Catching my eye everywhere I played
As wind from the sea the trees frequently swayed.
If I could go back, though, I certainly would
To play once more in the Tipperary Wood.
I've seen Muir Woods near San Fransico,
And travelled through forests by train to Moscow,
I've seen trees from Soeul to those at Doonfoot,
But none in my heart have taken root
Like those that gave my spirit elation,
As I played in Lord Annseley's little plantation.
In the Tipperary Wood we were a coastguard or smuggler
And across its little paths we chased each other;
And into the passing Shimna River we would wade
Like Tom Sawyer on the Mississippi ~ we'd got it made.
For the world was ours in that little wood
As on pine seeded carpet we often stood.
There we wished it were forever afternoon
Though the sun went behind the mountain soon.
Pink sunset clouds were high above us
And the tree tops almost dappled those clouds, cumulus
And I would go home to my mother's delicious macaroni
Or a centre loin lamb chop worth all its money.
And at 40 Bryansford Road I'd go to sleep
Serenaded by the song of the thrush and I'd meet
The Sandman again at Slieve Donard's foot
Where our little family had taken root;
And in the stillness I could hear the sound of the sea
Rolling in its nightly rhythms over me.

Willie was a forrester at Tollymore Park
Nature's beauty in his life played a very large part

Of a red waistcoat, a watch-and-chain and a fight

At the Gospel Hall on Shimna Road
We worshipped the Lord, in gentle mode,
And its people stand out in my memory tall
But the most vivid was Willie Small.
Yes, I remember wee Hammy Farr
And red–cheeked Mr. Rennox in his "Oxford" car;
And then there was Mrs. Willie Bloomer
And John, Joe, James and Willie Alexander.
I recall Auntie Gem and Mrs. Jordan,
And Mrs. Flynn, but, if they'll all pardon,
It's Willie I remember most graphicly of all,
Riding hatted on his bike to the Gospel Hall.
Willie was a forrester at Tollymore Park
Nature's beauty in his life played a very large part
At the former seat of the Earls of Roden,
Willie an outdoor life had chosen;
He often crossed Tollymore's rubble-built bridges,
Named Maria's, Foley's, Parnell's and Horn,
Ivy and Hore's and Clonachullion.

With the late Robert, Earl of Roden, Willie acquiesced
For the Earl on a stone had some words placed,
And those words to this day powerfully call
The visitor to "Stop, look around and praise the name of
Him who made it all".
I've met great theologians in my time
I've seen academic prowess, truly fine,
But, somehow, Willie stands out as a life marker for me
Standing in public reading Isaiah 53.
For we had open worship each Sunday morning
And Willie often started that worship's dawning.
He wore a red waiscoat with a watch and chain
And over the years he read that passage again and again;
It meant more to him than wealth or fame
Because it exalted the Messiah's name.
Sometimes I look on the great Van Gogh's famous painting
Of an open Bible, a candlestick and a novel, and thinking
Upon it I notice that the candle has gone out,
And the novel is well thumbed: what is it about?
"Joie de Vivre by Emile Zola" is on the book's cover;
Vincent, though, once gave himself to the other
Book in his painting, opened at Isaiah 53,
With every word he had agreed.
He had as an Evangelist once preached of the Saviour's glory;
His favourite hymn was "Tell me the old, old, story".
But the light had gone out of his evangelistic passion ~
Emile Zola was now more in fashion.
But Willie stayed closely by Isaiah 53
And the light of his witness still reaches me.
"There are no Mr.'s in Heaven" he would often say
As he helped folk put on their coats on a rainy day,
As they prepared to go home after a service
To the phrase "Thanks, Mr. Small" he was impervious!
He never liked to be called "Mr Willie Small"
"Willie will do" he'd say, with a smile to us all.

Every Sunday he gave me a single pound
Which bought each week's dinners in a school term's round.
It helped my mother get through for her money was scarce,
And she had precious little of it in her purse.
My life was now beginning to open up
And I drank from an even wider cup;
Surrounded by characters of all kinds
And teachers trying to stretch our minds:
Mrs. Lacelles whose crossed foot always stabbed the air;
Walter Martin whose many keys jingled down the corridor;
Mr. Archer who threw chalk all over the place;
And Austin Gibson or "The Buzzard", if you please,
Would our scholastic problems try to ease,
"Remember what it says on Ballygowan Clock," he would warn,
A truth I have learned to never scorn:
"The time is short" the letters read
A fact which cannot be gainsaid.
Of course there was the famous Kenny Rea
Who was head of PE in our school day.
"Give me the ball" he constantly said,
A statement which always went down just like lead.
One incident at school I remember so well
Of a fight with Ed Tormey, I must tell,
And of John Garland who held my coat that day
As Ed and I fought so viciously;
And of how we later became good friends
And very quickly made amends.
A nickname Ed gave me still makes me smile, though
He called me "Dericko from Jericho"!

As he cycled home along the Downpatrick Straight
His life ended before he got in his own gate.

Of a time to die and a time to speak

Since my High School days I still can hear
Washy Waterson's laughter in my ear.
But sadness, too, touched all our fun
When Sam Robinson was killed in the blinding sun,
As he cycled home along the Downpatrick Straight
His life ended before he got in his own gate.
I can still remember his head of black hair
And his clear complexion and his humorous air.
"There is a time to be born and a time to die"
Mr. Fowweather would read at the School Assembly;
For me it soon became a time to speak
Because one day Mr. Watts got me onto my feet
At a school debate where I made a speech
And on the strength of that he got me to compete
In a Debating Competition between schools,
Whose speakers certainly were not fools.
When I had some courage found
I asked what would happen if I won each round?
"You'll be doing your stuff in the Whitla Hall"
He replied and that was not all,
For he coached me in his "English" room

At lunchtime and, surprisingly soon,
His helpful advice greatly aided me
In the nuances of public oratory.
"Don't use your hands!" he firmly said
And I held them still and no progress made.
"Ach! Without your hands you couldn't speak"
He laughed as he tried to bring me to an eloquent peak.
But we got to the final, Norrie and I
And at Queen's University I heard students cry
With hilarious laughter as pennies they threw
At me, while I spoke, the motley crew!
I did my best to ignore them amid the commotion ~
"World Government is inevitable" was my debating motion.
 I managed to survive their demonstration
As I gave them thoughts from the Book of Revelation!
I came second and an adjudicating Professor told me why
(And I promise that I do not tell a lie)
"You looked at your notes", he firmly replied ~
If I hadn't I think I might have died!
The next year the School Debating Society I chaired
And "A" levels were attempted and I deeply cared
That to Queen's University I would go if allowed
To join that hilarious, motley student crowd!
I remember one quiet summer's afternoon
Passing out the school gate in the month of June
When I realized that as a pupil it was my last time
To walk out the gate of that school so fine,
And now, a whole new future I faced
Without those special people who had traced
Deep influences on my mind and heart
As on life's path I had made a start
And I felt a shiver of something bitter-sweet
Creep into my thoughts (for words far too deep).

Che Guevara was a T-shirt icon,

Of the times that were
a'changin'

"The times they are a'changin'" warned the song
That Dylan's voice rasped as the Sixties swept along.
He was right ~ for as Mao's Red Book emerged,
A wave of revolution across China surged;
And through "The South" Luther King marched on
With justice in his sights and freedom in his song.
In France the student protests went as far
As to lead their country close to Civil War;
Change came as Barnard transplanted a human heart;
At Woodstock 400,000 played a part ;
And Janis Joplin's "Cheap Thrills" album sold a million,
And Janis died at twenty-seven mainlined on heroin:
"I'm here to have a party, man, as best I can"
Said Janis, but, the party did not last long; and
Scott Fitzgerald of gifted 1920's literary fame,
Who gave Jay Gatsby his haunting name
In a book called "The Crack Up" had penned
Words about Hedonism's nightmarish end:

"The horror has now come like a storm", he wrote
Then added that there was "No choice, no road, no hope
Only the endless repetition of the sordid and semi-tragic."
He knew Hedonism held no lasting magic.
"All you need is love", the Beatles sang
As the vicious Vietnam War in Asia sprang.
And me? Through the late Sixties I was at Queen's ~
A University which by no means
Was untouched by the changing time
That swept across history's shifting tide.
Political fever touched our campus
And fences were challenged in political marches,
And Mary Quant's fashions were the rage ~
Donovan caps and white-booted legs.
Che Guevara was a T-shirt icon,
And the Six day war hero was Moshe Dyan,
And Harold Wilson smoked his pipe
While seeking to bring us economic light.

A passing taxi we enthusiastically hailed
And this time our enquiry did not fail
To bring us to a seat in a huge congregation
At the Baptist Church, to our spirit's elation.
I will never forget the obvious Christian fervour
Displayed as those Christians worshipped the Saviour.

Of the Great Hall and a
Czarist dress

I studied for a General Arts Degree
At first English, Economics and Psychology.
From Conrad to Skinner knowledge I sought
And of coffee in the Great Hall I drank a lot.
Those leaf falling days of Autumn closed in:
Hawthorns carried crimson haws in Aughlisnafin.
But Academia now gave demands for my mind
As answers to deep questions I tried to find.
One day an advert caught my restless sight;
It seemed so good it hardly seemed right:
"Moscow and back for 59 pounds"
Seemed an offer which did not often come around.
Gary Bowman and I agreed without a murmur
That we'd go to the USSR that summer;
And some of our friends came in tow
And Cold War shivers we came to know.
I remember crossing into East Germany by train
There was only one track as many miles we gained
Then I watched a military procession in Warsaw from up a tree
And unfortunately the branch broke under me;

A policeman then kept following me wherever I went
And I wondered if to a cell I'd soon be sent!
But he was persuaded by others to let me go
And imprisonment I didn't come to know!
In Moscow we were shown the treasure of the Czars;
Riches beyond any peasants reach, by far.
I remember seeing a dress of golden thread
That some Czarist dressmaker had delicately made;
Guides wanted us to know why there was a revolution
That to Czarist rule Russians had wanted a solution.
They showed us Lenin's life, depicted in a museum ~
It was obvious that they had a high view of him ~
And amongst the Young Pioneers that we were allowed to see,
There was a statue of Lenin with a child on his knee.
In the stadium they portrayed what Lenin said about sport
And in the Red Square his mausoleum held court.
To millions who viewed his embalmed body there
Guarded by soldiers with meticulous care.
"I don't believe in God", my guide firmly stated,
"I only believe in my family", his voice grated.
"But look Velodia what you have put in His place!"
I said, referring to Lenin's body in the glass case.
Velodia was not helpful in guiding us to a church,
But on Sunday morning we made our own search.
A passing taxi we enthusiastically hailed
And this time our enquiry did not fail
To bring us to a seat in a huge congregation
At the Baptist Church, to our spirit's elation.
I will never forget the obvious Christian fervour
Displayed as those Christians worshipped the Saviour.
We went back again on the Wednesday night
And somehow it just seemed right
After the service to gather folk around,
And as I played on the organ a beautiful sound
Rose from those Russian believers as they began to sing

In contrast to Communism's song so grim.
"How great thou art" was the hymn we sang
And, my, how gloriously those words rang
In the heart of that Church building in that Cold War day
In praise of Him whose word will not pass away.

As the guest of the Queen's Debating Society, our host,
He said, "How can I debate against the Holy Ghost!?"

Of Plato and the
Emmaus Road

As I pressed on for my general Degree
My faith was seriously rocked by Moral Philosphy.
My Professor was my probing tutor
And for the Christian faith he was no suitor.
"This is a very Christian essay", he proposed,
With his half-moon glasses on his nose,
And some of my arguments he would demolish
By his brilliant philosophic polish.
"Christianity breaks down in time of war,"
He would argue, with a look quite sour
As he chipped away at my faith's foundation
Amid huge moral shifts within the nation.
While studying Plato and John Stuart Mill
And Marx and Engels I found my will
To follow Christ was challenged day after day
By what philosophers had to say.
Did not Satre claim that in a godless world we choose
Our own values? His thinking clearly would refuse
To own that the claims of Christ held ultimate sway;
He said that we determine our very own way.
"We create ourselves", he firmly claimed.
Was the Christian faith, then, all in vain?

Or what about Albert Camus, Satre's friend,
Who said that, ultimately, in the end
Our lives have no significance in an indifferent world
And to claim that they have is just simply absurd.
It was all meaningless, he asserted
Which challenged the assumptions of the converted.
I particularly had difficulty with the Genesis story
Were Adam and Eve simply an allegory?
How could I really know that the Bible was true ?
Did I need to learn of a way that was new?
Then I rediscovered a truth which dispelled doubts gnawing,
Like the sun which darkness dispels at its dawning.
By faith I walked on the Emmaus road once more
Where millions have often walked before;
That road where Jesus at Moses began
And then throughout all of the Scriptures verbally ran,
Showing truths to His loved ones concerning Himself
It was all incredibly beautiful spiritual wealth.
My heart said, "If Jesus backed up the story of Moses
What matters what Philosophy proposes?"
Because Moses wrote the Book of Genesis in the first place
The book where Jesus Himself could trace.
I believed that Jesus is God's Son
And that His Word I could depend upon.
That word has held me all of these years
And has removed countless threatening fears;
And it is always inspiring to be able to say
That the same Word is definitely here to stay.
I also studied Political Science to boot
What a fascinating subject, getting at Government's root!
And then something happened in my final year
To direct my life into another gear.
I was walking down the steps of the Students' Union
And a sign quickly brought me to a firm resolution:
"Religion is a myth", the sign firmly declared
"What's this?" I thought, as my interest stirred.

The Debating Society were going to debate the motion
And suddenly my heart filled with deep emotion,
For the sign carried words provocatively put in
Which said "Jesus did not die for your sin".
"I must speak out against this", in my heart I said
And soon my path to the Debating Society led.
For seven minutes I spoke to that student crowd
And poured my heart's thoughts out aloud.
I did not have a religion but a person, I stated
As against the humanist John D. Stewart I debated.
"Christ is no myth" I strongly asserted,
And this time I was not primarily speaking to the converted!
I expected to meet with fierce opposition ~
Of that I thought there would be no question ~
But I was asked to represent Queen's in a national competition
It was called "The Observer Mace", but there was friction
For the motion I was asked to propose
The Scriptures clearly and plainly opposed:
"Marriage is no longer a social necessity" it said
Into "Free love" such thinking quickly led.
What was I to do? I must seek advice
So I went to see an academic who closely followed Christ.
"Are you going to use your gift for your own or God's glory?"
He said when I told him my debating story.
Dr. Gooding argued that people do not think very deeply to sin;
They are looking for an excuse without or within.
He said I could give them that excuse in my speech
For which I'd give an account when the Lord I would meet.
So I said a gentle "No" to the well meant invitation,
Learning that following the Lord is a challenging vocation ;
And yet He showed me by His gentle might
That His yoke is easy and His burden is light.
They asked me, though, to later take part
In the "Queen's Orator" debate. So I made a start
On preparing a speech on an interesting motion
Which gave me a quickly rising notion:

To try and declare where I truly stood
And to present the Gospel if I could.
The speakers lined up on that memorable night,
People whose careers would later take flight,
Like Nick Ross of later television fame;
And Derek Davis, who became an Irish household name,
Was our ever cheerful chairman that final year
As the time to leave Queen's began to draw near;
And Brendan Keenan whose very sharp mind
With others the "Queen's Orator" title sought to find.
"Students are a lost cause" was our debating subject,
And of huge heckling I became the object
As I presented my case, which in a nutshell
Said even students needed a Saviour as well;
That Christ was the answer to our need
And his message was vital for us all to heed.
In all of my life I have never faced
A more hostile crowd as upon me they laced
Verbal abuse and much derision.
Then the adjudicators retired to make their decision,
And finally about midnight they had made their choice
And one of their number gave their decision voice,
As to how they had finally come to agree
To give the "Queen's Orator" award to me!
I'm sure there were those who thought that decision,
Befitted nothing but their derision,
But Brendan Keenan said something tongue-in-cheek
In his runner-up speech later that week.
When the trophy was presented at the Wellington Park Hotel
And I recall his line so very well:
As the guest of the Queen's Debating Society, our host,
He said, "How can I debate against the Holy Ghost!?"
So my University days ended at the Whitla Hall
Where I got my degree and then life's call
Led me away from those days of debate
To a new path which God was about to create.

I love the story of C. S. Lewis saying his farewells
To a friend in Oxford, and that friend tells
That Lewis crossed the street and was then heard to cry
"Christians never have to say 'Goodbye'!"

Of giving Mary a kiss

My path in life now led to Lurgan College
Where pupils were pursuing all kinds of knowledge.
I most enjoyed teaching my "A" level pupils
And especially to listen to their various scruples
Regarding the morality of what writers wrote,
And the rapport was certainly far from remote.
We devoured what Arthur Miller had to say
In "Death of a Salesman", the parabolic play;
We read the great John Milton and the matchless Keats,
Whose nectar of words is a pleasure to secrete.
Though to try to teach younger pupils The Bard
Was always a challenge, and sometimes hard.
"Romeo and Juliet" was not a high priority
For Lurgan schoolboys, no matter what authority
Insisted that it was a truly vital part
Of learning Literature's great and varied art.
I had fun teaching Juniors Kenneth Grahame,
He of "The Wind in the Willows" fame.
With relish those children enacted Badger and all,
Fighting those weasels at the stately Toad Hall.
Imagination is not restricted by classroom walls
When good writing stirs and enchantingly calls.

And, of course, when poetry I tried to expound
Somehow, I could almost hear the sound
Of Norrie Watts voice lilting in my ears
Coming from those unforgettable Down High School years.
I found it hard to realise that it was my turn now
Literature's legacy to help endow
To young minds facing all that life brings
And to try not to clip Creativity's wings.
I want, now, for a moment, to recap
As the years across my memory lap;
As into my past I deeply delve
I find that I was preaching when I was twelve!
I was asked to speak at a service in Drumaness,
And, in my school uniform, I addressed
Those quiet folk in that County Down place
And of those faces that I can still retrace,
I especially remember the gentle Tom Lewis
(A former cricketer of some batting prowess!).
Through all my teenage years and while at Queen's
I tried to speak up for Christ, by all means.
At the Press Corner, on Dublin's O'Connell Street,
At Mountmellick in County Laoise,
And from County Galway to County Clare,
I tried to present the Gospel there;
In the Sandes Home in Ballykinler, where soldiers meet;
(They with raucous heckling a speaker would greet!)
Even in the Top Hat ballroom in Lisburn town,
Where a huge teenage outreach coffee-bar could be found.
Every week found me somewhere or other
Preaching Christ and the Gospel's answer
To the needs of the heart and of the hour
And proving its constant life changing power.
My mother was my constant source
Of inspiration on the Christian course.
Her prayers were awesome and her love was deep
And her humour through everything would seep.

"Give me a kiss, Mary" was her favourite joke ~
It maybe her courtship days evoked ~
"Give me a kiss, Mary", the fellow said
But Mary was not so easily led.
"Are you deaf, Mary?" the fellow pleaded
"No! But are you paralysed?" Mary acceded.
My mother's humour constantly permeated
The home which her gifts had created.
There was another Mary of whom my mother spoke
And into the Biblical story she helped me look.
"Mary choose that better part", she said with certainty,
"It won't be taken away from her for all eternity".
What I learned of Christ, she earnestly taught
And of His Word, if seriously sought
Would be mine, she would joyfully say,
When all of this world had passed away.
Such teaching came from a Christ-centred mind
Treasures the Holy Spirit had helped her find.
"What do you do with your newspaper the next day?
You light the fire with it", she would firmly say
And I often watched her spread a sheet of newspaper
Over the chimney's breast, and later
The created draught would make the fire blaze
And a cheerful flame would greet our gaze.
Journalism was transient, she would point out;
Writing for Christ had much longer clout.
The impermanence of every earthly thing
Was a theme which from her lips would often spring.
She believed that what was done for Christ would last
And that every earthly glory would eventually pass.
No fellow ever had a better mother
And her life constantly pointed to another:
That other was Christ, and the things He taught
And then came the cancer against which she fought.
I heard her crying night after night
Overwhelmed with searing pain in all its might.

Would that we could have assuaged that pain
As it stabbed in upon her again and again.
My Aunt Elizabeth was a gem with her nursing skill,
And she applied it with a loving will
"What's it like, Mum, as a Christian to be where you are?"
I asked and it was not going too far;
For she and I were extremely close
And for asking the question I have no remorse.
"See that text on the wall?" she said, pointing
It had been given by the Spirit's anointing
To Isaiah in a century now long past
But now it stood right in my mother's path.
"Thou wilt keep him in perfect peace", it said
"Whose mind is stayed on thee", it read
Then she gave me the Mandarin translation,
Which had given her spirit deep elation:
"You will keep him in perfect peace", she said
"Whose mind stops at God", she relayed.
"That is what I've got", she quickly expressed,
As the words upon my spirit pressed.
Then one day a message came as I taught my school class
That made me drive home to Newcastle, fast.
But when I got home my mother had gone forever
To be with Christ which is very far better.
So back to Drumee cemetery we sadly went
And the gravedigger's spade once more didn't relent
To cover death which is a curse, it is no lie ~
Only Christ's resurrection our last enemy defies;
And if trusting in Him, we can certainly know
A victory over death's cruel and heartless blow.
I love the story of C.S. Lewis saying his farewells
To a friend in Oxford, and that friend tells
That Lewis crossed the street and was then heard to cry
"Christians never have to say 'Goodbye'!"
It is true and as I think of my mother at rest
I say with Browning "With God be the rest".

Oh the joy of driving my first little car!
It carried me near and it carried me far.
It cost me only ninety four pounds
And it really helped me get around.

Of Glendilough and the road less travelled by

A woman now reached out to deeply strengthen me;
My vulnerability she could plainly see,
For I was alone and mixed with my many faults;
My emotional life was turning somersaults.
I was twenty five and though she had six sons,
She treated me as if I were another one.
She could have easily any need of mine disowned
But she took on my problems as if they were her own.
Her name was Peggy and with her husband Norman,
A business they were successfully forming.
It held a specialist place in selling concrete and sand,
Sending their trucks all over the land.
Of Peggy and Norman Emerson I could write many pages
For their zest for living was truly contagious.
They opened their home to me when my mother passed away
With its red brick welcome on the shore of Lough Neagh.
It was quite a family with whom I stayed,
And many incidents into their history fed.

Norrie as a child was heard to cry
As a rooster nearly blinded his eye;
George fell into the huge grit bin
But the Craigavon Fire Brigade rescued him;
Kenneth, once, nearly lost his hand ~
Emerson life was anything but bland ~
And Alan exhausted in his works aftermath
Was once found fast asleep in the bath;
Patricia in fun with her brothers would parry
And then left in order to marry Harry;
Geoffrey was a mechanic with a brain truly rapid
And looked after my Austin Mini's tappits.
Oh the joy of driving my first little car!
It carried me near and it carried me far.
It cost me only ninety four pounds
And it really helped me get around.
I have sat in jet aircraft around the world,
And crossed the Artic Circle where cold air currents swirled,
I have ridden in a Ferrari and a Rolls Royce,
I have paraglided on the Spanish coast,
I've helicoptered over the Statue of Liberty,
But none of these things, in reality,
Brought me more pleasure than that Mini car ~
It was truly a wee travelling star!
And Peggy cared for me with a mothering eye
Though I must have caused her many a worried sigh.
She cooked up on thirty sausages and seventeen chops
And fifteen eggs in one cooking hop;
She baked ten apple tarts in any one week
And her cooking was always a delicious treat;
She washed twenty shirts at one standing
And one morning as I headed down from the landing
I saw some formidable guns at the bottom of the stairs
(Was there something going on of which I was not aware?):
Patrolling soldiers had been invited in for a breakfast meal
Against Peggy's kindness they did not appeal.

Most Tuesday nights I'd be found in the pew
In Lurgan Baptist Church on Windsor Avenue.
We'd "Go to hear Willie" by the score,
And he always left me wanting more.
Pastor Mullan taught Scripture in a very personal way,
Applying it to the life we lived every day.
One night sitting in that Bible Class,
I got a call which simply would not pass.
I did not hear a voice or see any light,
But a question arose with impressionable might,
In my heart as I listened to that Pastor expound
Treasures in Scripture which he had found.
If I gave as much energy to teaching God's Word
As I gave to teaching Shakespeare, the thought occurred,
Would the Lord not use me to other folks blessing
Like the man who that class was now addressing?
At Grattan's petrol pump opposite Willie's home
The Lord started to single me out, alone.
As I would slowly fill my car with petrol there,
I would at that little home gently stare
And be reminded that Willie had once been a tramp
That God had worked in his life despite his being a scamp.
I remembered that a University education had been mine;
I knew that teaching English was good and fine;
But to whom much was given, the Scripture said
Was much expected, and for guidance I prayed,
Knowing that if God was calling me now
To teach His word, I should not bow
To what public opinion might say,
But to surrender to God's will and way.
One day the headmaster called me out of the blue
To his study where I was given a clue
Of the direction God was calling me
From Mr. Truesdale's simple plea:
"Mr. Bingham!" he said, "Have you ever thought
Of the Christian ministry?" and my mind sought

To find out why such a question came from such a man,
And I eventually realised it was part of God's plan.
"Is there anything wrong with my work?" I asked.
"Not at all", he replied and then he cast
The words which turned my life around;
Effective they were and deeply profound:
"The whole bent of your life is toward the Christian ministry",
he said,
And those words into my conscience fed.
The poet called God's Spirit "The Hound of Heaven"~
Well, he came after me, unrelenting.
When God wants us to do something for Him
He makes it clear that it is no whim.
We hear His call at almost every turn;
Its unequivocal demand is hard to spurn.
Spurn it we can but we will suffer loss;
Better to obey it and take up the cross.
Selfish ambition will to oblivion sink
But He can do above all that we can ask or think.
Picture me pacing the floor one memorable night,
The decision before me was far from light.
To and fro I paced with Peggy listening,
As Decision's emotion my heart was twisting.
Long past the midnight hour we talked
As "Glendilough's" floor I ponderously walked.
Then I decided my life to dedicate
To spreading God's word wherever it would take,
My feet or hands, my heart or head
Just wherever I was by the Spirit led.
Peggy urged me on with her wisdom and faith,
And I threw myself on God's infinite grace.
To Mr. Truesdale's study I returned
And a lesson there I quickly learned.
Before I even got a single word out
Or got to explaining my life's new route,
He asked "Is it the crossing of the ways?"

I affirmed that it was and that in coming days
I would be seeking in Christian ministry to serve
(A privilege which I did not by any means deserve).
He then made a very haunting assertion:
From another nation he had known a famous person
Who had been, in public, a great preacher, he added
(And then his warning came unpadded)
In private that preacher had been extremely worldly
And against such behaviour he gently warned me.
I sometimes think of that warning in that headmaster's room
It was good advice for all that faced me, soon.
In June, then, I came out of another school gate
And faced a new life of teaching the Christian faith.
Across the world and around the corner,
A life as intriquing as the former.
I remember, though, telling a certain Christian man
Of my decision and his words piercingly ran
Into questioning what I had done ~
In fact he broke my young heart with his tongue.
He meant well, I'm sure, but he didn't think
And his words made my feelings sink.
I reeled with the impact of what he said,
And that night a disturbing visit made
To my mother's grave opened eight months before
And sat on its edge feeling hurt and sore.
I then asked the Lord for just one thing ~
I asked that He would let me just one soul win
For Him in all of my preaching life.
And then came a lifting of that strife;
The sickening strife that was in my heart
Trying to rip my decision apart.
And as I gazed at the starry sky
I no longer had to reason why
For the door of new service was now open wide
And towards that door I began to stride.
I didn't know as I sat on Drumee hill

That God would lead me in His will
To one day broadcast His word from that sky
By satellite across Europe and he did not deny
The call He gave me, no matter what people said
I was, for His namesake, gently led.

Many came to Christ in answer to prayer,
Rising from the sincere people who gathered there.

Of the Chief Assistant to the King's physician

Variety is life's spice, they say
And I found plenty of it across my way.
To San Francisco I flew that summer
As I followed the sound of the distant drummer.
I preached in Oakland and I found
That the "Jesus Movement" was around:
Thousands of young people were turning to the faith
And the Spirit of God was moving apace.
One evening, though, I had to smile
For a statement my humour quickly beguiled.
I was sitting at a service one evening in Berkeley
And I heard this statement with absolute certainty:
"If you have anything to give put it in the collection basket",
The man said as he then quietly passed it.
"And if you need anything then take it out",
He added and his sincerity I did not doubt.
Now this differed from the services to which I went,
And in Ulster I wondered if such a basket were sent
Around a service would there be a theft,
And by the last row would there be anything left?!

A memory of that summer was an African-American singer ~
Will I ever forget her? She was a winner.
In the Anaheim Stadium to fifty-thousand folk,
Ethel Waters sang and in her words I soaked.
"For His eye is on the Sparrow", she sang with obvious glee
"And I know (Oh! How I know) He watches me".
He watched me too as back to Ulster I came
And soon the burning evangelistic flame
Led me to services at Ballyworkan,
About 3,000 miles from California, I reckon.
The Johnston family were so very kind
Their hospitality quickly comes to mind:
Stewart, Kenneth, Terry, Sally and Mrs. Johnston,
Whose commitment to Christ was keen and constant.
At their family home at Pepper's Trees I'd stay
Where herons flew and chestnuts lay.
Then on to Killeen near Armagh city
With my friend Bob Hewitt, gentle and Godly,
Where we preached the Gospel night after night
Across many weeks and before our sight
Many came to Christ in answer to prayer,
Rising from the sincere people who gathered there.
One Sunday we hired Shamrock Park Stadium in Portadown
And hundreds of people gathered around
To listen to the world's best news
On football stadium seats for their pews.
"Souls not goals" one man asked for in prayer,
As he committed the outreach to the Lord's care!
I've seldom seen such intercession
As spiritual needs before God were mentioned;
And God sent us answers week by week
As on our knees His power we'd seek.
I must mention one incident around thirty years ago
When a young student approached me, and I know
What he did deeply affected my whole career

And he did it without the slightest fear.
"Your preaching is too light", he challenged me;
"You need to go deeper" and this I could see;
"Come to Cambridge", he said, "As my guest"
And so I did at his kind request.
His name was Alan Gillespie and to him I owe
A debt far greater than he'll ever know.
He was the President of the Cambridge Christian Union,
And that week-end a tremendous fusion
Of spirit with a speaker turned me around
And sheer inspiration I happily found.
I got to the Cambridge Union and I still can see
An older man in his seventies walking by me.
He wore an overcoat and carried a little case
And wore ankle boots and his mood was serious.
Hundreds of students piled in to listen to him
And he had not come to speak on a whim.
"Were you late for the hockey match this afternoon?"
Was his opening line and very soon
Those rowdy students settled down,
As Dr. Martyn Lloyd~Jones started to expound
1 Corinthians chapter fourteen for well over an hour
With incredible, riveting spiritual power.
It seemed as if only fifteen minutes had gone
And I wished (Oh! How I wished) he had gone on.
As I sat there I knew what Alan had meant,
Deeper Bible expostion must now be my bent
If people were to be built up in their Christian faith
And helped to walk the path of grace.
The next day we had afternoon tea with the doctor
In a Cambridge tea room and all my life, after
I have remembered that expostitor in his prime,
Pouring God's word into this heart of mine .
On Sunday night in the Church-in-the-Round
I happily at the Doctor's feet was found.

Psalm 19 was his subject and again it seemed
That time was too short to cover his theme.
I told him of my desire to go deeper into God's word
And to teach a public Bible class, which he didn't think absurd;
But prayed with me and encouragingly said
"Go home and do it!" and so I was led
By God to that man and then our paths parted ~
His led to London and back to Ulster I started,
Never, ever to be the same again
Because of the vision which at Cambridge I'd gained.
Alan later become an investment banker with Goldman Sachs,
But when I look back upon the facts,
He gave me more than money ever could
By helping me to give out richer spiritual food.
The Doctor had once been Chief Assistant to the King's physician,
And could have been heading himself for his "Chief's position,"
But work with Lord Hodder had shown him clearly
That people needed more than medicine; merely
Their spiritually-sick souls needed The Great Physician's power,
And from the Christian ministry he did not cower,
But gave himself to it for the rest of his life
Backed up by Bethan his devoted and intelligent wife.
I shall always thank God that he focused on matters of the soul,
Encouraging me towards eternal goals.

That jewel of a place we love to this day.
The generosity of Margaret's parents helped us to stay
In beautiful hotels from Pitlochry to Skye

Of uncommon sense
and a luxury

Then Margaret came, vivacious, gifted and filled
With something in which she is highly skilled:
People simply call it "common sense" ~
But it isn't common and its effect is immense.
Self effacing, always a shunner of hype,
She walked into my life one Friday night
Within a few months we were engaged
To be married and our love was not assuaged
By her College studies or my public work;
And Margaret's open spirit did not shirk
The many new demands made upon her time
And to love her was a lasting luxury of mine.
In the summer of nineteen seventy one
I flew to the Far East with John Anderson;
Staying a night in Thailand's Bangkok
And then on to Soeul city and I never forgot
Climbing the hill to Pulwangdong
To be greeted by Korean Christian song.
And I left my shoes at the door
And sat with those Christians on the floor,
And rose to preach about "The woman at the well"

Who was offered living water and went on to tell
Of a Saviour who gave living water, still
To the "who-so-ever" will.
And a man in that service took a drink
Of that living water and I still think
Of my surprise at that conversion far from home.
I found, again, that I was not alone
But that the Spirit of God would always give me aid,
Just as Jesus had always said.
On that Korean tour I was preaching in a city
Called Anyang and I thought it a great pity
That the services were held in that burning morning heat
For most of my congregation, I thought, were asleep.
I talked with my interpreter, Mr. Kim:
Would it not be better, I suggested to him
To just stay with the services in the evening time?
The cooler air I thought was suiting us fine.
He felt we should continue and so I returned to speak
To that sleepy congregation in that heat.
As soon as I was finished a woman ran up
To where I stood and it seemed that her cup
Of life was just simply overflowing
For she was positively glowing.
And she hugged me tight and talked away
In the boiling heat of that Korean day.
I asked Mr. Kim what she was saying
As her language in my ear was playing.
He said that she'd come on the morning before,
And discovered that Jesus had died for her,
And she had trusted Jesus as her Saviour
The very first time the Gospel came near her!
And she had not slept the night before
Because of the joy that had come to her!
Ah! Was I glad I had prayed on Drumee hill
That God would let me win a soul in His will?

But I never dreamt that it would happen to me
With an eighty-one year old Korean called Yang Soon Lee.
Then came our wedding in June 'seventy four,
With the Ulster Workers' Council very much to the fore,
For they crippled the Province with their political stance
Creating hassle as our wedding plans advanced.
In the same month Margaret sat for her final examinations
In the midst off civil strife's contradictions.
The pressure was lifted, though, by an act of kindness
That came from a couple who reached out to help us ;
The Simms asked Margaret to stay in their beautiful home
Taking her from pressures that were burdensome.
They gave her space to study and they lent her a car,
And beyond the call of duty they travelled far.
Michael and Pauline lived at Terrace Hill by the Giant's Ring
And what they did for us was a beautiful thing.
Selfless acts somehow stand out as beacons,
Guiding our lives as we are seeking
To find our way through the labyrinth
And that beacon stands high on my memories' plinth.
After our wedding in Newcastle, County Down
We honeymooned in Scotland and travelled around
That jewel of a place that we love to this day.
The generosity of Margaret's parents helped us to stay
In beautiful hotels from Pitlochry to Skye
Where Highland heather grew and seagulls cried.
To Oban we sauntered and to Aviemore
But the best moment was to enter our own front door
And to begin our lives together at long last ~
It was unspeakable bliss to see bachelor days past.

"From my Window" my column was simply named,
And as its readership very quickly gained

Of writing for children
and atrocities

My work involved writing for children every week;
In The "Mourne Observer" hundreds I'd meet.
Mr. Hawthorne, the editor, kindly gave me *carte blanche*
And each week with my writing I'd also launch
A colouring competition or a puzzle to solve,
And my mailbox swelled as I would involve
Young minds from Annahilt to Annalong
To learn of Christ and salvation's song.
Jim Hawthorne was brave to give so much place
To Christian teaching in the face
Of commercial and social pressure to eat columns up
And I honour him for his constant help.
I miss him now on the Ulster scene
And his son Will who was also was very keen
To encourage me in the work which went on
It's still hard to believe that Will, too, has gone.
Winifred Gregg hugely helped me to get prizes around
To children all across County Down.
And we deeply appreciated the friendship of Granville Crory
He became an intrical part of our Newcastle story,
Weaving in and out of our daily round
With his TR7 helping to get him around!

"From my Window" my column was simply named,
And as its readership very quickly gained
A momentum and other papers ran it, too
Allowing teaching from a Christian point of view.
They included the "Armagh Guardian" and the Lisburn "Star"
And the "Northern Constitution" which even got as far
As Tamlaght O'Crilly and the Ballybogy Road
And thousands of readers now came aboard.
I know of one little girl who was eventually led to Christ
And became a missionary in St. Petersberg, who first
Had been influenced by that little column of ink
And a chat we had that had made her think.
I also remember speaking at Oxford University Christian Union
When a student approached me and in our communion
He reminded me that as a child he had been involved
In "From my Window"and at my home had called
To post his letter in my big red post box
His story truly humbled me a lot.
And families shared with us their sorrows and joys
As terrorists created horrors through thier many ploys.
Across a divided Province, it was a nightmare,
Yet in the midst of it all the Gospel we'd share
As Brian Irwin and I held many children's missions
And into many places were given admission.
Brian was as dedicated a Christian as I have ever known
As across the Province his musical gift was shown
To help children to Christ in an infectious way
As we missioned from Trillick to Killyleagh.
How can I ever express the joy we all had?
Children teamed out and were contagiously glad
To sing and sing and then sing some more
Of enthusiasm they had an unstinted store.
They listened well to the Bible story
In Ronnie Heron's barn, or down at Ahorey,
At the Iron Hall or over at Moneyreagh,

As we nightly taught that Jesus is the way
The truth, the life and the only Saviour,
Able to change destinies as well as behaviour.
The "Pilgrim's Progress" I just loved to teach
For Bunyan's wrting has huge power to reach
The imagination as well as the heart;
Great truth it holds for lives making a Christian start
It teaches how to get rid of the burden of sin,
And, how to overcome Appolyon and win
Victory even by alluring Vanity Fair,
And how not to succumb to Giant Despair,
And to know that the promises of God are the key
To bringing that giant to his knees.
That giant? He was busy in those busy years
For despair brought many scalding tears;
I remember John McConville coming to my home
For some counsel and he sat there alone
Telling me how he wanted to go to the mission field
And soon his future plans were revealed.
With Operation Mobilisation in Europe he'd serve
And high praise his dedication deserved.
But the hate of terrorists gunned him down
On his way home from work to Bessbrook town
Seven other colleagues were murdered with John,
And heartbreaking it was to go along,
To John's burial service, led by the Reverend Nixon,
Amidst huge communal grief and civil friction.
I remember that brave minister before the world's press
And a huge congragtion, rise to address
The grief in our hearts as those coffins lay
At the foot of that pulpit on that unforgettable day.
But tears overcame his attempt at words
As they flowed down it face, and, it occurs
To me that those tears said much more
Than words ever could as we sat by death's door.

And thirty years of it we were to endure,
Blasting our lives and making us constantly unsure
That we would ever come home from city or town
As many terrorist explosions erupted around.
I recall a girl I knew who had to have one thousand stitches
In her body caught within a bomb's reaches
Yet, before John's funeral I went to his home
And stood by his coffin in his bedroom,
And his Bible lay there in that scene of grief
And he had once written a statement on its flyleaf:
"It is the praising heart that can believe", he said
"Great things of God in prayer", it read
It was a praising heart that was muderously silenced, I thought
As those wicked people their victory sought.
At that time a church in New York, New York
Had my full time preaching services seriously sought.
Would I go, I wondered to those people and preach
At Calvary Baptist Church on West 57th Street?
As I came down that tiny little staircase
From John's bedroom, a piercing question now faced
My heart and mind with searing power:
How could I go to New York at such an hour
In my land's dilemma? No, I must stay,
And by God's grace, not go away,
But a real difference I must try to make
In a fractured land for the Lord's sake.
Fractured? One day I shook Brian Faulkner's hand
As the IRA's terror campaign was fanned.
I looked into the former Prime Minister's eyes
As hatred all decency had defied.
And murdered Maurice Rowlson just after he had kissed
His newly bathed six year old Cheryl and passed
Out his door to police duty and into his car,
And a boobie trap bomb took the good man far
From his wife Pearl and his child at home.

What heartless hand planted such a bomb?
And there the former Prime Minister stood,
With hundreds of us in sombre mood,
By the yew trees in St. Coleman's cemetery
With that young widow whose live was now so empty.
There are words, though, that come from suffering's cauldron,
And sometimes I seek to recall them,
For they inspire me, despite their obvious pain,
And they uplift my spirit again and again.
Facially wounded in a bomb explosion one day,
An explosion which nearly took his life away,
My friend David Lennox said words of note,
Which I now want to carefully quote:
"If God can bring order, " he said to me
"Out of the chaos of the cross," he added earnestly,
"Then He can bring order out of the chaos of my face"
And that comfort my heart can still retrace.

And Jock, the Scot, came every year;
He looked like Charlie Chaplin and, without fear,
The wee comedian would shake his collection box hard
As he walked around his audience: he was no coward,
And people would sometimes put small stones in ~

Of Pierrots, the "Broadway" and more terror

Newcastle Promenade, or, "The Front" was quite a place
As high summer days moved apace.
"The Pierrots" held their shows at the old bandstand
And they had a wide assortment of watching fans.
Their shows included Edwin Heath, the hypnotist,
And those summer crowds flocked with zest
To see what people would do under hypnosis ~
It was a disturbing voyeuristic process.
And Jock, the Scot, came every year;
He looked like Charlie Chaplin and, without fear,
The wee comedian would shake his collection box hard
As he walked around his audience: he was no coward,
And people would sometimes put small stones in ~
Poor Jock's collections, I reckon, were often thin.
People would line the Promenade wall for a better view
Of what was old hat and what was new;
And sometimes individuals would fall and take a tumble
To the sand and stones below, and would loudly grumble
Of the broken arm they painfully got,
For that show in the end had cost them a lot!
They would be taken along to Doctor Gibson's house,
Along with those who from hypnosis had not pulled out.

When I see that Newcastle bandstand now preserved from rust
In the splendour of Rowallane Gardens by the National Trust,
I know that if bandstands could audibly speak
That one would talk and its stories would peak
Any description I could manage to give
Of those summer days through which we all lived.
For many years there had been a practice
To hold open air evangelistic witness
On Newcastle Promenade, and my gentle father
Had in summer days often gathered
Crowds around him as he presented
The Gospel and had not relented
To preach its challenge and its good news,
Despite many surrounding and opposing views.
For years J.G. Hutchinson and Charles Wesley Fowler McEwen
Faithfully carried on what my father had been doing,
And a statement from Charles McEwen still rings in my heart,
And in my life has played a thoughtful part:
He said, "Sow a thought, reap an action"
(I can still hear his Devonshire diction);
"Sow an action, reap a habit," he said;
"Sow a habit, reap a character," he relayed;
"Sow a character, reap a destiny!" was his punchline,
And of this truth in life there's many a sign.
As time moved on I was asked to help lead
Those summer services and to spiritually feed
Hungry people, and God's help I'd invoke
To bring them into the fellowship of the easy yoke.
One needed moral courage which the Lord always gave
To overcome many critics talking, wave upon wave
And with my friends Rowald Pickering, Bob Hewitt and others,
I helped lead those services for eleven summers.
We hired an adjacent building on the Causeway Road ~
It was called "The Centre," and there we showed
Moody Bible Institute films called "Fact and Faith,"
And literally thousands of people heard the story of grace.

Charlie Knox was so faithful in helping us
To show those films nightly with no fuss.
It just broke our hearts when Charlie was killed
And his cheerful, helpful earthly life was stilled.
We miss Charlie with his ready smile
And that big trench coat he wore awhile.
I'm so glad Charlie good Christian service gave
But I never thought I'd have to stand by his grave,
And because life is short and eternity long
It makes Christian witness vital, as life moves along.
I think too of my friend Ronnie Heron
Who kindness and faith was constantly sharing,
And the incorrigible Hugh Lindsay who was not ashamed
To own His Lord and to exalt His name.
And Norman Mulholland, the ever cheerful Christian;
These have gone to their reward and there is no question
That they left a witness which now lives on
In the precious seed which they have sown.
My Uncle John, who lived next door
Was a mentor to me as more and more
Demands were made upon my preaching life
And his help was so encouraging and he gave great advice.
My Aunt Eleanor and he through many years
Were incredibly faithful Christian believers.
And Olive and Anne, my gifted cousins, were
Always helpful neighbours to have there.
On Saturday nights down at "The Centre",
We lit a big fire through the winter
And hundreds of young people came
To hear God's word and to praise His name.
There is one incident, though, etched on my mind's track
Of those open air services, as I look back:
And one evening Isobel Johnston took me aside
Without an ounce of spiritual pride,
And said, "Derick, I never thought I'd see the time
When you would preach with a son of mine

On this same Promenade where I used to be
A pierrot who did not like these meetings. You see
I used to whoop up my accordion to annoy
Your Dad speaking here on this Prom, and, boy
To think I would sit here listening to you two!"
I agreed it was certainly a very different view.
Isobel even sang with Sir Harry Lauder
And ENSA crowds would often applaud her
Then she found the Lord and got a new song
Which she truly loved as life went along.
And her son, George? I distinctly recall him speaking
On that Promenade to any who were seeking
To know peace with God and sins forgiven,
And that evening a text to his mind was given.
"Died Abner as a fool dieth?" cried George;
That message long in my memory will surge;
And one night death did come very close
And, believe me, I am not being merely morose.
For the IRA had a bomb in a moving car,
Taking it somewhere near or far,
When it prematurely exploded with a horrendous blast,
And from that open air service I ran fast
To find a young woman without a mark
On her body, lying in that bomb's aftermath so stark.
A nurse called Joan Nixon tried to save her life,
But death had come in the midst of that strife.
I helped lift a man's body from that road
Who was killed by the very terror which he had sowed
And we put it in "The Centre" outreach hall
We had on that road where they had nearly killed us all.
And I ripped down a curtain and covered that horrendous sight
And I'm still haunted by the memory of that fearful night.
Taking those services down at "The Front"
Wasn't always easy and I truly can't
Say we always had a lot of people to listen
As the sun on Dundrum Bay would glisten.

Indeed one day I was found at home to mull
Over the fact that I had just preached to seagulls!
But one service was by far the best
It was much more effective than all the rest
It happened at ten o'clock at night
And year after year it was an inspiring sight
To see crowds gather to sing God's praise
And many hymns and choruses they'd raise.
Sometimes it seemed that the moonlight on hand
Had created a silvery pathway to the Isle of Man,
Across the Irish Sea that lapped on the shore
As God's praises from many a heart would soar.
And to the "Broadway café" or to "The Strand"
They'd retire for supper or carry chips in their hands
Along "The Front" as the midnight hour came
And they'd return the next night for more of the same.

The next year along came Kathryn Ruth,

Of the mid-day sun, the North Pole
and new babies

While I saw many silver linings in Ulster's dark clouds,
The world, of course, kept on turning around.
History was constantly being updated:
The Yom Kippur war had many Israelies elated;
Then the Arab oil embargo crippled prices
And the Western world faced a huge oil crisis;
The Soviet Union then expelled Solzenitzen
Who had exposed decades of their ghastly prison system;
Patty Hearst joined in robbing a bank,
And America's Watergate cover-up stank;
Haile Sellasie ended a fifty-eight year reign,
And Margaret Thatcher began to make her political name;
Saigon fell to the victorious Viet Cong;
Jaquelin du Pre's sweet notes were by sadness strung;
Borg the "ice man" beat Nastasie at tennis,
And 800 million Chinese had a three minute silence
For Mao-Tse Tung, their leader who had died;
"Appolo" and "Soyuz" a new friendship tied
Of Russians and Americans as they docked in space,
A more mature action than the childish space race.

Margaret and I, though, took our own flight
Stopping in Hong Kong for a night,
And on to South Korea for a period of nine weeks
Where in a Seoul tennis stadium I nightly preached.
About three thousand turned up for the first meeting
And those Korean believers gave them warm greeting.
But a strange cult gave out leaflets saying I was one of them.
It affected attendance, but the Lord gave us gain
For we turned to radio and defied the Devil's opinions
And the programmes went out across a population of millions.
That programme continued after we were gone,
In Korean hands with Christian teaching and song.
Other services followed and many came to faith
For the Gospel is not bound by colour or race.
Bob Hewitt came with us on that tour
And taught the Scriptures superbly and his humour
Was a God-send in that oppressive heat
(Poor Margaret in the Chosun Hotel found a seat
And to that air-conditioned spot down in the city
She often fled from the sun that shone without pity).
Those Korean believers devotion to Christ and His call
Was something which deeply inspired us all,
And they encouraged me, too, to keep preaching on
In the land of that relentlessly boiling sun.
We stayed with Ulster folk at that time
And in those weeks we got along fine
With Billy and Mary Stevenson and Isobel
And Billy junior, and we could tell
God had done a great work in that family's life,
For Billy Stevenson had been in the heart of Ulster's strife.
From wrongful paramilitary activity he had turned away
To become a Christian, and I must say
Those Koreans loved him for his Christian work
And no bitterness in his heart now lurked.
I think the world of that family and applaud them because

Of their long dedication to the Christian cause.
It was a challenging, worthwhile and busy time
And in my mind I can see a thin white line
Along a table at Panmunjom,
In the Korean de-militarised zone,
Where North and South Korean officials would meet
At either side of the table they'd each other greet.
I was told one placed a flag higher than the other side
Who would then get one bigger, their enemy to deride;
And the flags got so big that very soon
They couldn't even get their flags into the room!
Ah! Not only in my country are there fights
But warring many a nation blights.
We came home the other way around the world,
And over the North Pole spectacular scenes unfurled
(Though if heat or cold were a choice for Margaret
She's take the cold any day for a trip to market!)
The next year along came Kathryn Ruth,
And I tell the absolute and honest truth
That of all the things I've ever seen,
Watching her birth in my story has been
The greatest mixture of fright and thrill and joy;
And although words I am trying to employ
To describe her birth, they simply fail
To capture how I truly feel
About that heart thumping, heart warming occasion
Of viewing that miracle of God's creation.
How can a father find words to describe
The birth of his own and very first child?
My first thought, though, was really very pleasant:
I stood wondering what I'd buy her for a Christmas present!
Then four days after her birth she took very ill
And our hearts with grief began to fill.
For she came very close to death,
And we all began to hold our breath

As a transfusion flowed from an unknown vein
To help bring her healthy life again.
To the Blood Transfusion Service we are deeply grateful,
And to the staff at the Craigavon Area Hospital
For the care they showed and the aid they gave
In order that our child could healthily live.
And to God we give all the glory
For bringing Kathryn into our life's story.
Three years later another baby was beginning to grow
In Margaret's womb and Doctor Victor Glasgow,
A friend and mentor, one evening asked
To examine Margaret and she was aghast
When he said she either had twins or a two headed child:
Her immediate reaction was far from mild!
Sure enough a future x-ray showed soon
Two babies waiting in Margaret's womb
To waken all our future lives up
And on to the family scene to erupt.
Three weeks later the moment of birth was reached
And they were both rather seriously breached;
And then came a man much, much larger than life,
Who became a permanent hero to my wife,
And not only Margaret but thousands of others
Give this gynacologist the very highest honours.
For if Jim Dornan told Margaret to stand on her head
She'd do it and not fell falsely led!
With his famous humour and legendary skill
He safely delivered Claire and Kerrie, and still
Margaret speaks of him to this very day
For his infectious attitude and inspiring way.
What a man! Our Province is certainly a better place
Because Jim has our maternity wards paced.
And those two babies turned our schedules around
And as soon as Margaret's feet hit the ground,
She coped magnificently in meeting their needs

With sleepless nights weaving around constant feeds.
We found with twins there is a golden rule:
They did not like any interruption to their schedule.
So we learned to keep them around home for two years
And stopped trying to fit our schedule into theirs!
And were they alike? I'll say they were,
For one day Margaret was heading out to the Doctor
When she saw something that truly shocked her
In her arms she thought she had a twin who was ill,
But suddenly she cried in a voice that was shrill,
"Oh! I've got the wrong one!" she cried to me
Though that fact was not really easy to see!

On that same trip I was in New York, one day
And was walking on the Avenue of the Americas with Billy Jay,

Of a Bible Class and a
New York sparrow

I sat one day on Belfast's Botanic Avenue
With a teacher called John Graham making a review
Of an invitation which he had brought to me
Which had great spiritual potential, it was plain to see.
John represented the leaders of Victoria Memorial Hall,
In which a church had met for sixty years in all
Down on May Street in Belfast, where it had held witness
To Christ and His Gospel and now saw the fitness
Of a new location on University Road
For the church to meet in a new abode.
The leadership wanted me to seriously seek
The Lord in prayer about trying to help meet
The spiritual needs of a rising generation
As a new witness began its incarnation.
I left that meeting with John, challenged in my heart
About the work in which I would soon play a part.
Then in the coming weeks the vision began to rise
To establish a Bible Class which would highly prize
The pure word of Scripture to all who would care
To listen to its wisdom and its light to share.

I met one evening in Victoria Memorial Hall
With a group of the elders and all
Listened as I tried my feelings to impart
And we agreed that we should soon make a start.
Mr. William Agnew said, as I headed for the door
"Will you give us twenty years?!" and I gave one more.
For I was privileged to serve twenty one years as a Bible Teacher
With the Crescent Church and that class was a feature
At the very heart and soul of my life,
Through many years of incredible sectarian strife.
Tens of thousands of people came across the years
For the comfort of Scripture amid their fears.
In good times and bad, God's Word held us steady
When Despair was always at the ready
To crush our hopes and spoil our vision
And our Christian faith to have in derision.
One summer I was sitting in a bus in the State of Georgia
Beside my friend Val English on the way to Florida,
When he suddenly urged me to consider
Teaching Christ's Sermon on the Mount and to deliver
Its incredibly varied and rich spiritual food
Right into the heart of Ulster's mood.
I baulked but Val very quickly mentioned
That the rest of the New Testament was just an extension
Of what the Sermon on the Mount had taught
As those people Christ's priceless wisdom sought.
Val's encouragement to me has always been
Warm, cheerful and wise, and from what I've seen
Of the working out of the things he's commended
His insights have deep service rendered
To my life as I have seriously sought
In the will of God to tentatively walk.
He is the most versatile pastor I know
And to his hearth I'm always happy to go.
On that same trip I was in New York, one day
And was walking on the Avenue of the Americas with Billy Jay,

A joyful Welsh Christian who never thought it odd
To see in everything, the hand of God;
And right in the middle of the traffic's roar
I heard something amid those skyscrapers that soar:
It was a little sparrow chirping, perched on a traffic light
And, as soon as my eyes lit upon the sight,
Billy claims he knew exactly what was in my mind
And he was right, for it was not hard to find
The message God was giving to me that busy day
As that joyful little bird chirped away.
And together we stood and worshipped the Lord, there
On that busy Manhattan throroughfare,
Knowing that God cared for us all like that little sparrow
No matter how wide our circumstances or how narrow.
I had to smile at Billy, though, on that tour
For as we went around the White House he was not demure
In saying that he thought the wallpapering was well below standard;
And that it was not the quality of work deftly handled
With the Cardiff City Council by he and his squad:
White House wallpapering he certainly did not applaud!
(A fact, though, remains in history forever
That it was an Ulsterman from Rostrevor
Who with his troops burned the city of Washington
And ate the hastily abandoned dinner of President Madison
In the White House in 1814;
With an appetite which was extremely keen!
But I'm not sure if Major General Ross, when he called,
Noticed the papering on those walls!)
Val was right, of course, about the Sermon on the Mount ~
He knew what he was talking about.
The Bible Class attendance across the weeks
Surged to eat the spiritual meat,
We found in the Sermon on the Mount,
And only Eternity will truly account,
For what was accomplished as Christ's sermon was raised
Tuesday by Tuesday before our hearts' gaze.

It moved me deeply as week by week
We studied the sermon of the "Turning of the cheek".
"Tuesday Night at the Crescent" became part of many lives
As the work of God continued to thrive
And people came every week
Setting their hearts and minds to seek
The treasures of truth found in the Bible,
Treasures which are truly unrivalled.
In other work the Crescent Church brought
Outreach and witness as it sought
To serve the Lord in South Belfast
As the years of our lives began to run fast.
After two years as a family we moved,
For the Lord did not allow us to get in a groove,
Though to leave the Mountains of Mourne for a city
Was quite a decision in the nitty-gritty
Of life, but what we did I do not regret,
And over that decision I do not fret.
At thirty three and a half years of age I left behind
The Kingdom of Mourne where you can find
Nature spreading puffballs, ceps and shaggy ink-caps;
Where you can walk up Deer's Meadow and the Hare's Gap;
Where you'll find the Brandy Pad and Butter Mountain
And drumlins by the thousand for the counting;
Where you'll see the Rowan Tree River and Slievemageoh
Or Crocknafeola, but, we had to go:
Still, a word of Hugh McBirney's lingers on my mind's track
He said that 'the sound of the water' would bring me back!

I felt led to speak on the twenty-third psalm

Of Filey and a Cockney prayer

I had a friend who felt deeply in his heart
That it was time for me to make a start
To move in service to a wider base
Than up to this time had been the case.
Eric Clarke felt I was restricting what God had given to me
And needed a wider Christian ministry.
So he recommended me as a speaker for "Filey",
The Christian Holiday Week which was held yearly
In Yorkshire at Sir Billy Butlin's huge holiday camp
Upon which six thousand Christian's made their stamp.
They took it over for seven days ~
It was just incredible to see the ways
They turned that holiday site around:
Overnight in the huge bar was found
The largest Christian bookshop in the country
And the camp radio was now playing, to all and sundry,
Christian music and the Butlin's staff were amazed
That six thousand people were not phased
By alcohol not being on sale.
Year after year those crowds never failed
To flock to those Bible studies and sing God's praise.
My friend Eric Clarke used to powerfully raise

The special music rendition of the Lord's Prayer
With thousands of human voices, there.
In the Gaiety Theatre on my first morning
I faced three thousand people, and, it was daunting
As I stood in the largest theatre in the United Kingdom
And how I needed tact and wisdom
That morning when I first rose to speak
To those hungry folk in those tiered seats.
I felt led to speak on the twenty-third psalm
And soon came to the verse as I moved along
Which describes death as the Valley of the Shadow
And this description, of course, is not shallow.
For if there is a shadow, there must be a light
And no matter how powerful or with what might
An enemy may approach us, the fact remains
If only the shadow touches us, we will retain
Our life and we will have a future
And on this truth my audience I tried to nurture.
For the light in the valley of death is the Saviour
And He will guide very single believer
Into the glory on the other side,
Where millions of the redeemed we'll find.
Now it so happened as I was speaking
Stewards moving in the aisles were desperately seeking
To find a woman in that listening crowd
Whose husband had just suddenly died.
He was to travel from Scotland that afternoon
And she had of course been expecting him soon
But as I was explaining the twenty-third psalm,
Jim Harper was experiencing Heaven's calm.
Janette, his wife, went home in grief,
But later on in that memorable week,
She sent a letter which the Chairman read to us all
And its contents our hearts deeply did enthral.
She wrote of the comfort she had received

From that teaching on death for those who believe,
And she said she felt the Lord had sent her that morning
To prepare her for Jim's death and a warning
Came to me as I heard that letter read.
For if the truth be honestly said,
I had struggled with the fact that the crowd might declare
That the twenty-third psalm was too lightweight fare
For such a time and such a place
And I learned there a truth to face:
That the message God gives is relevant
And will always accomplish that to which it is sent.
I think of those fascinating teams of people who were
So gifted by God as they ministered there,
And later on when we moved to Skegness by the sea
Their various gifts worked harmoniously;
Sheila Walsh and Amy Grant sang of Christian hope
With Graham Kendrick and the gentle Dave Pope;
Alan Redpath was there and the Godly Tim Buckley;
Stephen Olford came and the inspiring Ian Barclay ~
Shall I ever forget Ian teaching each morning
From the majestic Songs of Solomon?
Focused leaders like Gilbert Kirby and Norman Sinclair,
And others like Rosemary Harris were very particular
That the right balance be struck to help those huge crowds
To be spiritually fed and have their lives turned around.
For me, one of the most memorable times I've known
Was to teach what the Lord had shown
To me from what the Bible said,
Of the friendship that David and Jonathan made.
Over a thousand young people came each day
To hear what the teaching had to say.
Privileged I was to be part of it all
And as its joyful memories I recall.
To people like Lindsay Glegg I glad tribute pay
Who saw after Billy Graham's great meetings in Harringay

That thousands of young Christians needed help
To go on to know the Lord in greater depth,
And had started "Filey" with huge vision
(Now continued in Northern Ireland at the yearly 'New Horizon').
How we need such visionaries to have the courage
To lead Christians work and who do not worry
About the obstacles that are set in their way
By the Evil One who wants to hold sway,
And to block any outbreak of Bible teaching and praise
By any barrier he can possible raise.
Of course there is always something to bring a smile
And there was one incident in my memory's file:
It occurred when at a prayer meeting in Filey,
When a prayer was made in a mood somewhat wiley.
A gentleman leading the prayer meeting bade us keep
Our prayers short as soon we must meet
Our audiences at the appointed time
(And to be late would, of course, be a crime).
Suddenly a man stood up to pray
And in a Cockney accent I heard him say:
"Lawd! I don't know who this bloke is," he began
"Whose telling us 'ow to pray", his words ran
"I don't care who he is," he said as he gave his view
"I'm not praying to 'im, I'm praying to You!"
I confess that I certainly opened my eyes
Who was this man who my sensibilities surprised?
"Oh, that's Fred Lemmon," I was told when I asked
And from Fred many a pointed prayer passed.
He was converted to Christ in Broadmoor prison
And the converted burglar certainly saw no reason
To "hang about" in any of his prayers,
Taking to the Lord his petitions and cares
But getting right to the heart of things, immediately
In words of one syllable, often hilariously!

So Eric Clarke was particularly used by the Lord
To "enlarge my coasts" in the work of God.
And amongst other churches I began to preach
Beyond those of my youth and tried to reach
Hearts with the finest of the wheat
Of spiritual food, their hunger to meet.
And it was with the deepest pleasure
I saw response beyond what I could ever measure.

And although his attention I did not seem to keep,
He was, in fact, deeply interested in sheep!
The word of the Good Shepherd, through John's Gospel,
touched his heart
And the Holy Spirit's conviction began to start

Of the Princess of Wales
and Marie Wilson

The world was now entering a new decade
And the nineteen seventies were beginning to fade.
Outside No. 10 stood the woman from Grantham,
Making the prayer of St. Francis her anthem;
"Where there is discord may we bring harmony", she stated
"Where there is despair may we bring hope", she related.
Many years later I met her one day
In the House of Lords and I have to say
I found Baroness Thatcher as fascinating face to face
As her premiership, which would deeply impress
Her views and personality on the nineteen eighties
As she responded to politics entreaties.
Discord she faced and despair, for sure
And for the world's ills there was no easy cure.
Pol Pot slaughtered millions in Cambodia's killing fields
And the Ayatolla took his American hostages;
Lord Mountbatten was slain in a County Sligo nightmare
And the Pope was shot in St. Peter's Square;
Blank shots were fired at the Queen in the Mall.

President Reagan was wounded outside a Washington Hotel;
President Sadat faced a cruel death, so stark;
And John Lennon was murdered in New York;
Sikh bodyguards shot Mrs. Indira Ghandi;
And the priest, Populuiko who backed Solidarity
A cruel and heartless death met
For standing for freedom against the Communist threat.
Margaret and I had, one evening, agreed
To have supper with some friends and our gifted MP.
But that afternoon terrorists murdered him
And the killing of Robert Bradford was a blatant sin.
Was it any wonder, then, that seven hundred million people
Turned their eyes upon St. Paul's Cathederal,
To watch Lady Diana Spencer marry Prince Charles
Hoping that romance was again at large?
"It was the stuff of fairy tales", said Archbishop Runcie
And we all wanted to believe it, I fancy.
Princess Diana always makes me think of the words of a song
Which she epitomized as her life moved on.
They are words which describe her personality's enthrall
And from her island grave they still seem to call.
The sentiment that the words of the song state
Is why those tons of flowers were laid at her gate:
They say "Reach out and touch somebody's hand
Make this world a better place if you can".
Despite what anyone says about the Princess
They can't deny that with remarkable deftness
She reached out and touched so many hearts and hands
And brought comfort and hope to millions in our land.
She often brightened our lives, that candle in the wind,
And her indelible contribution no one can recind.
Diana and Charles soon had to travel to Enniskillen
To try to comfort hearts after the fearsome killing
Of thirteen innocent lives by the IRA
And amongst the slain was precious Marie.

She was a member of my Bible Class
And for no better daughter could parents have asked.
We had once been studying the letter of James in Scripture,
And Marie had made that study a weekly fixture.
She had made notes of what Scripture was saying to her
As its power her heart would often stir.
When Marie's effects were eventually returned
From the Royal Victoria Hospital as her parents mourned
Marie's notes from James were found by them;
Her mother wrote and told me that, time and again,
Deep comfort from those notes were gleaned
In the midst of all the tragedy they had seen.
And of course her husband by his attitude
To those whose action, so heartless and crude
Had taken Gordon Wilson's daughter from his side
Touched millions, and, his beseeching words
Against terrorism and its tenants, so absurd
Carried huge weight in the eye of the storm ~
His example gave peace body and form.
A headmaster had once kindly invited me
To speak at Enniskillen High School and from what I could see
He was deeply anxious that the Christian message
Would touch his pupils as they began life's passage.
He was an inspiring and very thoughtful person
And to help him I needed no coersion.
On Remembrance Day he finished teaching his Bible Class
And made his way to the service at Enniskillen's Cenotaph.
When the bomb exploded the masonry around him caved in,
And except for one gloved hand, completely buried him.
The next day he slipped into a coma at two p.m.,
And he has been in that coma for thirteen years on end,
Cared for daily by Noreen his incredible wife
Who daily hopes for a miracle in his life.
To such sorrow what does Noreen say,
As terrorism's legacy touches her day after day?

Is she bitter? No, for "Bitterness is a very hard burden to carry"
She states, and, with it will not parry.
"Vengeance is for the Lord, I can leave that to Him"
She says, in the face of man's cruelty so grim.
Such a woman as Noreen truly epitomizes
Faith, and not mere philosophic surmises.
During three decades of "The troubles" in Ulster I've lived
And in the population one in every 400 was killed,
And one in every fifty was injured here ~
That all our lives were affected is perfectly clear.
I even remember, once, preaching at Ballyhackamore
And a bomb went off near the Gospel Hall's door.
As windows came in upon that seated congregation
We faced a truly horrific situation.
Raw terror I saw upon all of those faces
And of the terror of that night my mind still has traces.
Despite all of our troubles, though, we gathered around
The Word of God, true, powerful and sound,
On Tuesday evenings and the subjects varied
As God's message through His Word was carried.
"Does God still guide?" was a practical series;
"Doubt ~ a faith in two minds" answered some of our queries;
"A spiritual spring clean" was one of our studies;
"Insights from John 10" lifted many worries.
From one man in particular who came along
Though at first he was bored with the preaching and song.
He counted the organ pipes (37 in all!)
And the Word on hard ground seemed to vainly fall.
But it was not so. Joe Morrow was "brought up on the land",
The youngest of thirteen he was sadly orphaned.
Born in County Donegal, his school he would greet
With reluctant stride and tiny bare feet.
He eventually arrived, though, in Belfast city
And there are few undertakers who are more witty!
And although his attention I did not seem to keep,

He was, in fact, deeply interested in sheep!
The word of the Good Shepherd, through John's Gospel,
touched his heart
And the Holy Spirit's conviction began to start
To reveal to him his need of a Saviour
And his conversion day began to draw nearer.
And one day at Portstewart while he was on holiday
He surrendered to Christ and went on solidly
To live for Him and to give vital service
As Tuesday Night's chief steward, and, I am not nervous
To say that Joe would prove to be
One of the most helpful people you'd ever see.
He found hundreds of people their seats on Tuesday nights,
Took an interest in them all and kept me in his sight
And cared for my needs until the last light went out
Because late night counselling was often what we were about.
His sense of humour is truly something else
And of a fund of stories he has huge wealth.
The most famous is the one about the graveyard preacher
Which in Joe's conversation is sometimes featured:
Joe was undertaking at a burial service one afternoon,
When the preacher was determined not to finish soon
But went on and on, his timing was truly awful.
So the gravedigger went up to him and handed him his shovel
"Fill it in when you are finished", he angrily said
And to the preacher's sermon he quickly put paid!
Many a smile Joe and I had amid serious work
Something, believe me, he has never shirked.
And to Joe and his wife Lorna I owe a lot
As the greater glory of God they together have sought.

Yet bravely fought at Alamein for your country;
And you truly played your focused part
In seeking to root Nazism out of Europe's heart

Of Tomintoul and the lamplighter

In all public speaking it is vital to remember
That one fact applies from January to December:
It is that you never know who is listening to you
Be it on the media or even in a church service pew.
Margaret, a superb cook herself, took me one day
To hear what a famous television cook had to say,
And as I listened to Michael Smith at the Culloden Hotel
I tried to learn a lesson and to learn it well.
Michael told how he was making custard one day
Before a discerning audience, and, in his own way
He decided to joke about powdered custard;
And he wasn't shy or even flustered
In saying "None of your Bird's Custard here"
And didn't know his words had fallen on Mrs. Bird's ear!
When they told him, at the break, of his *"faux pas"*
He then returned and apologized; he had gone too far.
And he laughed and stated that he should have said
"None of your Brown and Polson's" instead.
The only problem was, as he later discovered
Mrs. Polson was in his audience and his bluff was uncovered!

Another principle I have learned and wish to emphasise
Is that often I did not fully realise
What my audiences were going through
(Though they sat so quietly in those pews).
One Tuesday evening at my Bible Class
We learned something we must not let pass.
We gave each person a piece of paper,
And then the stewards collected them all, later.
After folk responded to my request to write down
A problem which they had currently found
Troubling them in their hectic lives
As life and its pressures they tried to survive.
In the service later on that evening
I read out each problem and the meaning
Of my behaviour soon became clear:
It was to show that hundreds in my audience from far and near
Had some huge problems and it would have been hard to guess
Such problems in such an audience would exist.
At one stage we took fifteen nights in the Book of Job
And spiritual treasures in our hearts were stowed
From what Job learned in all of his trouble
Of the providence of God and, we were able
To learn that all that happens is not good, for sure
But all things work together for good and valuable lessons endure.
Our studies also took us down the road
Of the life of Abraham, the friend of God.
Through Proverbs we studied deeply to see
The wisdom by which we could all be
Wiser people as the century moved on,
Striving not to become secularism's pawn.
One series of studies truly proved itself
To be hugely inspiring and full of spiritual wealth:
We looked at every mention of the eagle in the Bible,
A bird which simply has no rival.
And those crowds as they came? I can still see them
Looking at the stuffed golden eagle from the Ulster Museum

That accompanied me in the pulpit, and it made
A very inspiring teaching aide.
By the kind suggestion of Gordon Brontë
(Yes, a special member of the famous literary family)
Recordings began to be made of Tuesday night teaching,
And soon thousands of tapes were quietly reaching
Across the world with the word of life,
Despite all our local sectarian strife.
And Gordon's son Alan and Gordon's wife, Dorothy
With the dedicated help of their friend Joe Skelly,
Organised and helped a team get those tapes out
Far and wide and around and about.
My own wings in the eighties I began to spread,
And particularly to Scotland I was led.
Quite often I visited a church in Motherwell
And as usual I could easily tell
That the Scots and Irish have affinity
Of a common Celtic identity.
They have the same sense of humour and directness
That does not stand on ceremony's correctness.
In Motherwell I had Willie and Sheena Moreland as my hosts ~
Willie, with vision, always made the most
Of every opportunity to reach out for his Lord,
With flair and big-heartedness in creative accord.
He taught me much about taste in Christian publicity
For which he had a natural felicity.
He always put out material that was first class,
That even Sattchi and Sattchi would have passed.
Sheena, his wife, had the most challenging mind-set
Regarding a healthy lifestyle that I've ever met.
I wish she would write about what she knows,
And she is a perfect example of a lifestyle that glows.
Believe me what I write is not mere sentiment ~
It's a lifestyle from which many would benefit.
Not everyone, of course, would necessarily agree
With what Sheena in the supermarket sees:

"Pornographic food" is Sheena's description
Of photographs of food found in lots of directions
 In many a large supermarket's Food Hall,
Giving the consumers pocket many calls!
In health we are what we eat, that is for sure
And Sheena's diets would many illnesses cure.
I started to preach across Scotland in depth
And over the last twenty years I have found myself
Teaching the Scriptures from Tillicoultry to Aberdeen
And from Lerwick to Kirkintilloch and in between;
At Maddison and Kircaldy and up at Thurso, too
And at Airdrie I rich fellowship knew
With Willie McClachlan and his friends
And at Riverside, Ayr on many a weekend
From the Goods and the Buntins and the Houstons and more
I knew much kindness and spoke to folk by the score.
Donald and Isobel Donnachie I will never forget
And the talent of Jack Martin who always set
An inspiring tone before our worship began
With a specially chosen piece played on the organ.
We recall with affection the Godly elder, Ian Mutch,
Whose life was lived with a gentle touch.
Is there anything more splendid than a drive past Denure?
And the view out to Arran gives stress a cure
And, of course there's a run backwards up the Electric Brae,
A mystery about which lots of folk have their say.
Further along the coast comes the castle at Culzean
And I tell you I do not speak in vain
That if you want what Elsie Good calls a "civilised cup of tea"
Have one at the Turnberry Hotel, looking out to sea!
At Milngavie, at Stornoway or Peebles on the Tweed,
I've had the privilege of sowing precious seed.
Now that my mind is in a Scottish mood
How can I ever forget "Lynwood"?
The former home of Stephen and Carol Cordiner
Nestling in pines at Deeside, yonder.

And the fun we all had with our Kathryn, Kerrie and Claire,
Who played in the little stream that flowed there.
As Kathryn turned her head to go to sleep
She heard some yodelling that made her heart leap,
For Stephen had placed a mechanical device
That triggered recorded yodelling and in a trice
Our children were out of their beds with hooting laughter;
It was yodelling they remembered forever after!
Ah Stephen! what a man you were.
You were so cheerful and you really cared
To show kindness to all and sundry
Yet bravely fought at Alamein for your country;
And you truly played your focused part
In seeking to root Nazism out of Europe's heart.
One day Stephen was driving me near Ballater
And said "See that wooded hill over there?"
"My father owned that hill", he said feelingly
And then he enchantingly explained to me
That with the hill, for the Cordiner's, there came a pew
And I found it fascinating news,
That the pew was at Crathie Church where the Queen,
Going to worship can often be seen
When at Balmoral when she holds court;
Queen Victoria's favourite place, of course.
As we looked at the former "Cordiner" hill
Laughter Stephen's mouth began to fill.
"Come to think of it", he said as we surveyed the view
"My Father owns all the hills!" which was absolutely true!
And, of course God owns the cattle on a thousand hills too,
And all the stars in the firmament, which are not few;
And all Creation comes from Him
Who created the very hawthorn in Aughlisnafin.
We picnicked as a family amid the Highland heather,
With Stephen and Carol in glorious weather.
Stephen made it possible for us to have his timeshare
At Abernethy Outdoor Pursuits Centre,

Run by the inspiring Lorimer Gray and his team,
Reaching many for Christ in that Highland scene.
As we set off for our holiday at Abernethy
With a very excited little family
Stephen said "We'll go with you as far as Tomintoul",
And they did, and of tears our eyes were full
As we waved our farewells. In a few short years
I climbed the stairs and shed more tears
At "Lynwood" for my friend was dying,
And on his bed I found him lying
Near, so near, to the Valley of the Shadow,
At the end of a life that was not shallow.
He cried and I cried and then I told him the story
Of the lamplighter, as he neared the Glory:
"Are you not scared in the dark?" the lamplighter was asked.
"Not at all", he answered, as the question was grasped.
Now lamplighters went out an hour before dawn,
To put streetlights out before the day came along,
And lamplighters went out, of course, in the darkest hour
A time when fear has increased power.
"When one light goes out", the lamplighter said,
I keep my eyes on the next one", his point he made.
"And when that light finally goes out
Keeping my eye on the next is what it's about.
And when the last one goes out, as I move along
Why I find myself in a glorious dawn!"
"The last light is flickering", Stephen said,
And soon into his funeral service hundreds were led,
But into that glorious dawn of a new day
Stephen Cordiner had already walked away.

By his compassion for those who were without
And as founder of Tear Fund he gave clout
To raising millions for those in need

Of the Dead Poets Society,
Keswick and George Hoffman

There is a place, which stirs the senses;
It enfolds the watchful traveller with joy, relentless;
In moonlight or sunshine, in fog or mist
Its mountains and lakes each other kiss.
It is called the Lake District but the word is too plain.
District? This place is more a kingdom and not in vain
Did Wordsworth say, "An intermingling of Heaven's pomp is spread
On the ground which British shepherds tread"
Even Dove Cottage at Grasmere, Wordsworth's home
Is described by him in words of idyllic tone;
He called it a "Little nook of mountain ground
… the loveliest spot that man hath ever found".
This kingdom inspired De Quincy and Coleridge too,
And Robert Southey with their Romantic view
Of life and nature in their heart
That in English literature has played such a part.
Romanticism? What does it believe?
What tenants of truth does it perceive?
It believes in optimism, enthusiasm and faith
And through mere materialism cuts a swathe
(For some people are so poor, in fact
All they have is money along life's track)

The Romantic believes in the individuality of each person
And if sentiment makes its own assertion,
It does not smother it cynically to death
And it never despises tenderness.
Of course Romanticism is often despised
Because of heartaches, which in life suddenly arise.
One of those heartaches came to William Webb-Peploe
An Anglican clergyman who knew deep sorrow
Standing by the graveside of his little child
And over his heart ran emotions, wild.
But he read a text from a Bible chapter
Which changed his attitude ever after:
It said "My grace is sufficient for you"
And William said "Lord, let your grace be sufficient, do!"
But a voice his attitude seemed to quiz
It said "How dare you ask God to make what is!
Get up and take and you will find it true."
And this truth turned his life around, anew.
Prebendary Webb-Peploe for over forty years
Was part of a Lake District Convention not far from Windermere.
It was held in Keswick by Derwent Water,
And from eighteen seventy five and after
The Keswick Convention has over many summers drawn
Hundreds of thousands of people who depend upon
The teaching of Scripture to nourish their souls
And who set their sights on spiritual goals.
Romanticism has its attractive beliefs
But, as in Webb-Peploe's crushing grief,
The assurance of faith in the swell of life's storm
Is better than anything in any form
And it is the best guardian of Romanticism's best tenants;
Better if the heart flies Christ's glorious pennant,
And a living hope will fill one's life
A hope one will never bury amid life's strife.
In modern culture I think of the film "Dead Poets Society"
Which has Mr. Keating trying to bring Romanticism's variety

Of thinking into the lives of the boys in his English class,
And "Pittsy's" enthusiasm takes it up; alas!
It leads him to despair and suicide.
I believe, ultimate peace one cannot find
Without taking on the easy yoke of Christ
Which is the lightest burden one can know in life.
Yes, I'm a Christian who believes in the ultimate romance
Of the Christian faith that can make the heart dance
With the joy of knowing all sins forgiven
Through Christ's atoning death and resurrection.
Over the years to Keswick came champions of the faith:
D.L. Moody and Hudson Taylor that platform would grace;
Bishop Taylor-Smith and Mr. Grattan Guinness,
G. Cambell Morgan and the great Captain Wallis,
Dr. Harry Ironside and Bishop Handley-Moule,
And Dr. Graham Scroogie would feed the souls
Of those who came from all over the world
As the banner saying "All one in Christ Jesus" unfurled.
My greatest "Keswick hero" is F.B. Meyer,
Who one evening stood before the audience, there
And expounded Biblical holiness before that crowd.
And when the next day came around
The local Post Office found that it had a problem
For after Meyer's teaching, with import solemn,
The Christians were paying their bills by postal order
And soon the Post Office couldn't find another!
After two World Wars came a new generation
Of Bible teachers who went to Keswick by invitation.
People like the writer-bishop Frank Houghton,
Dr. Stephen Olford and George B. Duncan;
Dr. Donald Barnhouse, Francis Dixon and Skevington Wood
Stood before those thousands in teaching mood.
Then came John Stott and J.Glen-Owen,
Richard Bewes, Raymond Brown and Michael Baughen,
D. Stuart Briscoe and Alistair Begg
These Christians gave to doctrine legs

And feet with the Holy Spirit's mighty help.
Then one morning I found myself
With a letter in my hand from Philip Hacking,
Inviting me to speak at Keswick and soon I was packing
And heading into that hallowed place,
Seeking to teach God's word by His grace.
Over the years I have returned with joy
To serve with those gifted colleagues in sacred employ,
And to fellowship with those thousands who meet
In that special place on Skiddaw Street.
One great memory, though, will always remain
Of a gentleman in a cravat and again and again
His words often come back to me as life surges on.
He was a dynamic Christian called George Hoffman
Deeply involved in helping the world's poor,
And often our hearts he would deeply stir
By his compassion for those who were without
And as a founder of Tear Fund he gave clout
To raising millions for those in need
Whatever their backgound, whatever their creed.
"One person cannot change the world", George would say,
"But you can change the world for one person", and, if I may
I'd like to pay tribute to George for all he did
As he sought of deep poverty to rid
Areas from Calcutta to Bosnia and the South American steppes
For he tried to reach out to those that wept.
One year at Keswick I had to get up early
To travel back home and I needed to catch a ferry.
"I'll have breakfast with you", George kindly said,
And early next morning the table was spread
At the Lairbeck Hotel and we chatted and talked
And he stood waving at the window as I finally walked
To my car and slowly drove away,
Hoping to see George on another "Keswick day".
But it was not to be for in an accident he was killed
A short time later, and my heart was filled

With grief at the loss of such a gifted Christian brother
As George, we will not find another.
At his memorial service at All Soul's, Langham Place
In London, tribute was made to his Christian grace
And it was truly and sadly bitterly-sweet
To see a film of George playing on some overseas street
With a child, as he carried out his mission
Of taking aid to the poor with his Christian compassion.
Ah! When the Lord returns and gives the call
The dead in Christ will rise first of all,
And those Christians who are alive and remain, here
Will be caught up together with them to meet the Lord in the air.
Then again I shall talk with my dear friend,
And of that eternal state there will be no end.

It was a study of the most incredible man
Who ever stood on Egypt's burning sand.
Joseph, the man who determined to put God first
In the highest of societies and who did not thirst
After position or fame or even money
And who never chased any empty glory.

Of mistakes, providence and the schoolteacher of Annan

Let me pause on this journey to review
A principle I've known which is not new.
I've made many mistakes in life, I'm afraid;
I've said many things I wish I'd never said;
I've hurt people by sheer selfishness;
And I've found action without thought hard to redress.
For one thing is certain, when all's said and done
Life certainly does not get a second run.
Within that fact, though, another is clear,
And I find it removes the onslaught of fear:
It is that doing God's will is not like a travel agent's itinerary ~
For in accepting that you know, even as a preliminary,
That if you miss a train or a plane on that list
You'll only get a holiday that's second best.
Believers all miss or disobey God's will at times,
But that does not mean that they will find
That they are second-class believers because of their faults ~
No, God draws out of his providential vaults
Ways to get them back into His will
And thus His great purposes to fulfil.

God turned Moses, famous for his wrath,
Into the meekest man in all the earth;
He transformed Abraham, the man who lied
Into a man of faith who quietly defied
The calls of the immediate for the eternal,
And he became known as the Father of the faithful;
God has used the repentant David's pen
To comfort millions, again and again;
And few would have imagined that the broken Peter
Would be restored to his Lord and then, later
Would write two New Testament letters of hope,
Which have helped untold multitudes to cope.
So, what word would I use to cover this life of mine?
"Privileged" is the word that comes to mind:
Privileged to know people like George and Pat Harrison
And their children Philip and Ruth and Jonathan;
Privileged to teach a Bible Class in Manchester city
And to stay with the Harrison's in their home in Worsley;
To know the young people who came to those meetings
On Friday nights, we'd give each other greetings
And then study God's word together in depth
Finding there, as always, spiritual wealth.
And our family recalls glorious days at Carr Laund,
With our friends the Palethorpes on their croquet lawn,
And the fun we all had on holiday together
Is very hard in words to measure!
Sarah and Jane and Eric and Joyce
Gave us friendship which was choice.
Privileged were we in having Tom and Grace Clark as friends
I actually stayed with them for over eighty weekends,
As in downtown Glasgow I taught a Bible Class
And they showed me kindness more than I could have asked.
The Class met on St. Vincent Street in "Greek" Thompson's Kirk
building;
And we were amazed to find hundreds of young people filling
That beautiful Kirk ~ it was like speaking in the Parthenon,

And I can still recall the passion of their song.
I remember one night giving teaching on the Bible's Tabernacle,
A subject, which is truly fascinating to tackle.
"Something happens when you teach it", my friend Professor
David Gooding said,
"Heaven comes down" and one night after I prayed
And closed the teaching with a hymn, there
In over nine hundred people there was not a stir.
Silently they sat on in the Kirk, gripped
As in their hearts "Heaven's dew" they sipped.
"Did you notice that silence?" I said to a young person at the end
"Aye! You want to savour it", he quietly said.
How can I ever thank Tom and Grace Clark,
Whose love and kindness in my life made its mark?
In all of those years I taught that Bible Class
Not a disagreeing word between us passed.
Sheer Christian dedication in their lives I saw
(And Grace, by the way, makes Scotland's best coleslaw!)
I used to fly to Scotland via 'Logan Air'
Though I often called it 'Logan-scare'
For as those little planes rode the turbulence above the Irish Sea
The experience often brought the perspiration out on me!
The Bible Class was called "Highway One",
And it was for eleven seasons to run.
Eventually we began in Glasgow's large Gaelic church to meet,
A beautiful building, which was hard to heat.
We brought in huge "Gas blasters" which hotly roared
Bringing heat which could not be ignored.
Overseeing those studies in Glasgow city
Was the Godly Jim Hopewell and his helpful committee,
Including Tom Clark, Joe Munro, Eddie Bradbury and others
Who their Saturday nights would freely offer
To the service of that Bible Class
That taught God's Word that will never pass.
One evening I was speaking in the English-Scottish border
When a Scots lass approached me, when the service was over,

And she told me about how she had found the Saviour
One evening at "Highway One" and then, later
She had settled in Annan as a schoolteacher
And I was so glad God's Word had reached her.
With shades of Samuel Rutherford I can truly say
(Only he spoke of Anwoth further along the Solway)
When that schoolteacher of Annan meets me at God's right hand
"My heaven will be two heaven's in Emmanuel's land".
Of the Eighties, though, one gem among gems remains
In my treasure of memories as time on me gains:
It was a study of the most incredible man
Who ever stood on Egypt's burning sand.
Joseph, the man who determined to put God first
In the highest of societies and who did not thirst
After position or fame or even money
And who never chased any empty glory.
Over those nights of study I can honestly say
God spoke to us in the most remarkable way
About the dignity of that young man faced with obscurity,
Yet when raised to influence and faced with promiscuity
Refused and suffered for his moral stance.
Through prison God his cause advanced,
And soon Pharaoh said no one would lift hand or foot
Without Joseph's word: God's providence was about.
Though Joseph became Egypt's Prime Minister,
No selfish pride or anything sinister
Ever marred his work or stained his witness
For all he faced, God gave him fitness.
We drew nectar from Joseph's inspiring story
As a new decade came upon us slowly;
A decade, which would change European history forever
And many of Communism's chains would at last be severed.

Some thistledown settles on Joylon's moustache, so gently,
Whiter, much whiter than the moustache and eventually
The stable clock strikes the quarter past,

Of a seismic crack, palaces and thistledown

Nineteen eighty nine was one of those years
When history moves into another gear:
An unknown young man stood in Beijing in June
Before a moving column of tanks and soon
His act of defiance won admiration across the world
As the Chinese pro-democracy movement unfurled.
The Chinese army ruthlessly advanced on Tianamen Square
Shooting at will and climbing over bodies, there,
And from cold brutality there was no release
On Beijing's Avenue of Eternal Peace.
Something, though, was stirring across the earth:
Communism was proving to have brought a dearth
Of the freedom of speech, of movement, of faith,
And in October East Germany's Erich Honecker fell.
Sixty thousand Hungarians heard their acting President tell
Of the birth of a new Hungarian Republic, in fact
And on Marx and Lenin, Hungary turned its back.

Then cracks appeared in a Berlin wall ~
Were they really and truly cracks at all?
They certainly were and they symbolized
A seismic crack in a system, I never surmised
I'd see in my lifetime, but come it did;
And then in Praque democracy made its bid
And two hundred thousand people held sway
In Wenceslas Square and heard Alexander Dubeck say
"We have been too long in darkness"; it was quite a sight,
Then Vaclav Havel and he toasted the light.
And Ceausescu fell and Romania breathed again.
Soon the very Kremlin began to feel the strain
Of finding that it certainly was no joke
What Solzenhitsyn had written about the calf and the oak.
In July Margaret and I drove through Buckingham Palace gates
And joined The Queen and her seven thousand other guests
At a Garden Party, and, I vividly recall
When we came to the final minutes of it all:
We and Earl Spencer were amongst the last to leave
As the crowds began towards The Mall to weave.
On that hot summer's day, I can still see him stand
Sampling a cake or a sandwich in his hand,
And I'm strangely reminded of a haunting piece of writing
By the gifted John Galsworthy where he is describing
The death of Joylon Forsyte on a summer's day
As an era of the Forsytes passed away;
An afternoon where bees seem to be saying "Summer-summer"
Where there was the soothing scent of limes and lavender;
And old Joylon is out sitting in the garden, drowsily
Quietly waitng for the arrival of Irene,
The "Indian summer of a Forsyte" Galsworthy calls the Section,
Some of the most powerful writing in fiction.
Some thistledown settles on Joylon's moustache, so gently
Whiter, much whiter than the moustache and eventually
The stable clock strikes the quarter past,

And now the thistle down no longer moves, at last.
For Joylon's breathing has stopped under the tree's shade
And "Summers lease hath all too short a date", Shakespeare said.
The Earl of that Buckingham Palace day
And his daughter, the Princess, too, have passed away,
And I had watched the obvious affection between them
That afternoon before thousands from all over the kingdom.
Ah! Life is fragile, so fragile like that thistledown
On the gentle summer's air as it floats around.
The old evangelistic hymn is so accurate
Speaking of the fragile nature of life, even in spate ~
For it is true that "Fairest flowers soon decay"
And that "Youth and beauty pass away."
It warns that we have not long to stay
And that in trusting Christ there must be no delay.
Once on a trip to the Isle of Man
I was staying with the Chief Constable and our chat ran
To talk of the Royal family and Robin Oak,
Of a man called "Milky" Williams spoke.
He was nicknamed "Milky" because he had been a milkman,
And rose to be a police officer with élan
To serve at Buckingham Palace on security as a detective
A position in which he was quietly effective.
One day in the Palace grounds "Milky" and King George VI met
And a conversation ensued which "Milky" would never forget.
The King was very ill and was approaching death
And found it very difficult to catch his breath.
The King spoke of "Going home" ~ what could he mean?
His home was all around him, plain to be seen.
But the King was referring to Heaven, a more permanent place,
Than any home found among any earthly race.
Through the King's witness "Milky" was converted
And was found often to have asserted
That King George VI led him to Christ,
The King of all Kings, with whom he made tryst.

Life moved apace too in my own ministry,
As I watched history unravel and people break free.
The huge Soviet Union crumbled in nineteen ninety one,
And John McCarthy was released from the Lebanon.
That summer I found myself deep in Romania's heart :
In Bucharest I discovered the frightening part
Played by Ceausescu toward the Christian Church
Against which his regime gave many a cruel lurch.
And I saw the incredibly stupid People's Palace, storey on storey,
Built by Ceausescu for his own empty glory.
And in the esplanade leading to the Palace,
I entered a buidling where, with cruel malice,
The Securitate had tortured Pastor Richard Wurmbrand
And now, by the Lord's almighty hand,
He and his friends had opened a Christian centre,
Selling Bibles and books and printing Christian literature.
There I found a man who was seventy years of age
"I feel younger since I came to work here", said the Romanian sage,
Then looking at his Hidleberg printing press, he said
"We bought this from the East German propaganda office!", (no less!)
"What do you put it down to?" I asked
He answered "He who sits in the Heaven's shall laugh".
And I think for the first time I could really understand
What that Bible verse meant, and the esplanade, grand,
Almost seemed to echo on that Eastern European day,
With laughter that came from far away.
Of all the most memorable situations in which I have spoken,
It was on that tour with my friends Tom Lewis and Tom Lawson,
When I rose to speak to a thousand people one Sunday afternoon
In the city of Arrad, and very soon
I found myself in an extraordinary situation which I did not seek
For my congregation suddenly began to weep.
Heart rending sobs filled that large church building
Where those thousand folk were quietly sitting.
Pastor Doru Popa, my translator, gently signalled to me

To stop speaking for a little while, and I could see
God's Word had touched a nerve in those Romanian hearts,
Who for long with pain and misery had been torn apart.
What was my subject on that extraordinary day?
It was a look at what the Scriptures had to say
About the intervention of God in the time of Esther,
When God intervened to save her people from disaster;
And how from the Red Sea to Bethlehem, God had stepped into time
It is a clear and definable historical line.
And, of course, the greatest intervention happened at the Cross,
A display of God's love, most incredibly wondrous.
There Christ's death opened the way back to God's heart
And from there the repentant sinner can make a start
Along that narrow way that leads to life,
Despite history's revolutions and cruel strife.
Then, after a time I began to speak again
And saw that the Scriptures did not say in vain
That against the church the gates of Hell would not prevail,
Though often her witness would suffering entail.
She would despite her sorrows eventually win through
As those precious people in Arrad were proving anew.
One day that summer I was walking in a Romanian street
And the dust was rising around my feet,
When I heard some children singing a beautiful song
In English as I passed along.
The words they sang still reach out into a new century,
Which I have just entered and I know eventually
All history will prove their inherent truth,
It will all be unravelled through time, forsooth:
"Our God is so big, so great and so powerful", they sang,
"There's nothing He cannot do," the words rang
Over that wall and into my heart and mind.
Those words, for me, now honestly define
What happened through those amazing days,
As God again displayed His mysterious ways.

And I think of friends who offered in a Russian newspaper
A John's Gospel to anyone who would write in, and later
They received over two million requests from hungry minds ~
Ah! it's true that only in Christ can we find
True living water on our life's course;
All other satisfactions will eventually dry up at their source.
And I now turned to serve the Lord in a new decade
Knowing that in Christ my true fortune was made.

He explained that the cause of their restless walking,
Came from years at sea, and he was not mocking,

Of Geneva, Matamata and the men of Findochty

I was in Geneva soon after the Berlin wall came down,
And in the Palais de Nations I was shown around
The UN headquarters by the Swiss Correspondent of Reuters,
And he pointed out to me one of his computer's features:
It was that a little bell appeared if a major story broke.
When to the news of "The Wall", the world awoke,
Bells started appearing all over his screen
As a turning point in history was clearly seen.
In that beautiful city in Switzerland one morning
I was invited for a media interview by a lady, who gave warning
That if I made a mistake there would be no edit:
"It will go out as a mistake", she said and yet it
Turned out to be a spiritually significant time
As Ginna Lewis opened up, with heart and mind,
With questions which she poured out that day,
And the Lord helped me in what I had to say.
The radio programme was called "Freely speaking"
And even with the Dali Lama she'd had a meeting
On her programme and it now happened to be my turn.
And a principle I would again learn:
I must not worry whenever such situations came
To witness to the honour of Jesus' name.

Jesus taught that his followers would be given what to say
By the Holy Spirit, come what may.
After many questions the broadcast's end was in sight
And Ginna asked me to sum up my message, if I might.
Then she launched into a description of Geneva's population,
Drawn from almost every corner of God's creation;
Representatives drawn from the Vatican to Afghanistan
Lived in the city and my mind ran
To that Bible passage so favoured by Willie Small.
Could I read it? Ginna did not mind at all.
So I read of how we like sheep had gone astray,
And how we all had turned to our own way;
I read how Christ was wounded for our transgression ~
The unshakeable basis of our redemption ~
And that by his deep wounds we are healed
(A truth sadly from many concealed).
Isaiah fifty three had inspired the forester of Tollymore Park
And it was my privilege to read it to the heart
Of one of the great cities of the world,
Where warring nations for peace have turned.
Later I turned to the "Land of the long white cloud",
Where hot mineral pools and bubbling mud can be found;
Where snow capped mountains soar into blue sky,
And glaciers and fiords and surging rivers defy
Words to describe them for their natural beauty
Though to try, I feel it is sometimes my duty.
Exotic and full of visual splendour,
New Zealand is a place I'll long remember,
Particularly Matamata in the Autumn light:
It seemed to be bathed in sepia; and the sight
Of a little newspaper shop with copies of "The People's Friend"
Amused me, there, near the world's end.
New Zealand's Britishness was truly fascinating
And one evening I went to speak at a Maori meeting,
And one of the leaders gently asked me, on the side
If I knew Willie John McBride!

Even Irish rugby heroes are much noted there,
Where the "All Blacks" are like gold dust in the culture.
Yes, I even panned for gold dust in Octago, at will
And managed to discover a flake near Invercargill.
What Christian writer would not at sometime mean
To have the privelge of crossing the Silverstream,
In order to visit the little town of Mosgeil,
Where F.W. Boreham showed his great writing skill
As an essayist; the man who first enchanted me
With the romance of Christian service in his biography.
When I read it as a struggling teenager,
I never dreamt that, many years later,
I'd visit the first pastoral environs of that majestic soul
In whose writing I would cast my mould.
Seventy one times I preached on my last trip,
In that memorable land on the Pacific's lip.
And to Malcolm Barrow who arranged my itinerary
My thanks I offer for the detail, extraordinary
With which he planned my speaking tour
That included the Tea Pot Valley and Rotarura,
Hastings, Auckland and Lower Hutt;
And I dined on oysters not far from Bluff;
And of the fruit of South Island I could not have enough.
Press and radio opportunities came across "Kiwi" land,
Where in the North they have a near fifty-eight mile beach of sand.
I also spoke at Marton, Queenstown, New Plymouth and Gore
Eventually coming home via Singapore.
When I think of New Zealand, I think of water, I'd say
In pool, in river, in ocean or in some quiet bay;
Playing on or in water across the whole community
Is New Zealand's supreme outdoor activity.
Water, I love it,in its many forms,
Particularly when it falls frozen in snowstorms
In the form of trillions of gentle, silent snowflakes
And each one a different pattern makes;
And raindrops falling on my head

Never ultimately to the blues have led.
I've seen Irish rain fall tens of thousands of times ~
It's the source of the deep green of the Emerald Isle.
As a child in summer I often swam in the sea
Or in Newcastle pool which surely must be
One of the coldest swimming pools in exsistence,
Against which we children put up stout resistance.
And often, still, to this very day
I swim with pleasure, and I must say
If there was water, water everywhere
It would not cause me too much care.
But the Book of Revelation teaches that in the future state
There is "No longer any sea", it simply relates.
Why, in the new earth should this phenomenon be
Is a fact which truly surprises me.
Then the men of Findochty opened my eyes
And I now see that in the phenomenon lies
Spiritual truth which comforts me,
Truth learned at Findochty, by the sea.
Findochty is a fishing village on the Moray Firth,
One of the most beautiful stretches of water on earth.
In the early nineties I sometimes spoke in Buckie
At a satellite Keswick Convention, not far from Findochty.
One afternoon the Church of Scotland minister, the Rev. Bill Ross
Asked if he could show me something and I was at a loss
To understand what I saw there by his kirk on the hill -
It was a sight of older "sea-salts" walking, strangely, at will.
They would walk over from the kirk to the hill's face,
And then together their steps they'd slowly retrace.
Again and again they'd repeat this walk,
Then another would join them and they would talk.
"Notice how they walk at an angle like a horse up a hill
They are walking up their boats", said the Rev. "Bill".
He explained that the cause of their restless walking,
Came from years at sea, and he was not mocking,
But explaining a fact. When I eventually got to bed

I slept on the phenomenon to which I had been led,
And as soon as I woke I thought of the Scripture
That spoke of no more sea in the forever after.
I thought of how the Bible says
That the wicked are restless in all their ways.
They are "like the troubled sea" the sacred text declares,
Always on the move here and there .
So in Heaven since no restlessness will exist,
There will be no more sea (if you get my gist!).
I spoke of my theory to the Buckie Convention that morning,
Explaining how my thinking had its dawning,
And afterwards a lady came to talk to me
About something she could clearly see;
"By the church!", she said, "You want to be in my front room,
Where my father simply never sits down.
When his mates join him, for he paces the floor
Up and down, over and over".
What a strange phenomenon to discover!
And in the Royal Albert Hall in London, one evening
I preached the Gospel, and, with feeling,
Choirs from all over the country sang a song, there
With their hosts, The London Emmanuel Choir.
It spoke of "Rest beyond the river" ~
May the men of Findochty know it forever!

Meanwhile, at home through those years it was pleasant
To have as an anchor at "Tuesday night the Cresent"

Of the Chaplain to the United States Senate, keeping up with the Joneses and the indominable Mrs Green

Life's shifting sands were shifting visibly,
As my life moved on with its responsibilities.
"It's a funny old world", said Margaret Thatcher,
As the "men in lifeboats" swiftly ditched her.
How swiftly it happened was pertinently displayed
When in her autobiography I sadly read
That on her very last day in office,
When she went to her study with final purpose,
She could not get in, what a sickening thing
For the key was already off her ring!
In Europe, Lech Walesa, the Gdansk electrician,
Had proved himself to be an astute politician,
And now he became Polish president -
Democracy had become a Polish resident.
Soon the flag of the USSR
Came down over the Kremlin and political power
Came away from the Communists, and Gorbachev resigned.
To Margaret Thatcher's credit, history will find,
A lot of praise is due her for the crucial role
That she played in fighting for the heart and soul

Of Democracy's freedoms in the face of constant threat
From those of a communistic mind-set
And even her own life was almost taken
By an IRA bomb in the town of Brighton.
The next threat on the scene was Saddam Hussein,
Another dictator rising yet again.
The Gulf War erupted against Iraq,
A trouble spot always threatening at the West's back.
And sadly in Rwanda so many people died ~
If only the international community had tried
To intervene in the midst of that horrific war,
They could have saved a million lives and more.
Politics has always interested me,
And I studied Political Science at University.
Yet in the Book of Daniel I have learned,
As far as the kingdoms of earth are concerned,
Whether democracies or dictatorships arise,
Seeking to lead a country to some glittering prize,
All of them are like the image in Nebuchadnezzar's dream ~
They all have feet of clay and it is plainly seen
All of them carry a flaw that is fatal
Even from Democracy's Grecian cradle;
It's that all of their promises they cannot ultimately keep,
Though many try and many seek
To keep as many as they possibly can
From Capitol Hill to Hindustan.
Only the "Ancient of Days", as Daniel shows,
Will establish an eternal kingdom and, Heaven knows,
To Him will be given power and dominion.
No matter what differing earthly opinion
Rises against Him, the Truth He'll defend
And of His kingdom there will be no end.
If he makes a promise he will deliver
And nothing his purposes can sever.
I proved this one day in Washington,
As on Capitol Hill I was walking along

A corridor, and, I asked direction
To the House of Representatives. The person
I asked, just happened to be
The Chaplain to the United States Senate, who said to me
"Tell them you've been talking to the chaplain, at the door,"
The Lord used that meeting to lead to more
Than I could have ever thought,
And soon an interview I sought,
And one snowy morning I talked to Dr. Lloyd John Ogilvie
For the "Belfast Telegraph", and, amazingly,
When the facts of his early life I tried to seek
He said his mother had raised her family on five dollars a week!
It was at the height of America's depression
And out of the schedule of his school lessons ,
Lloyd was what was then known as a "Soda jerk"
Selling ice-cream in a store, outside of school work.
At the age of thirteen his voice was broken,
He wanted to leave school and he was not joking.
Life was miserable and one day in the store
Where he sold ice-cream, a man came in the door
And asked if he might have an ice-cream.
"What flavour do you want, sir?" Lloyd asked and didn't dream
The impact of that question and what it would mean.
Lloyd happened to have his head in the fridge at the time
For he was cleaning it out, and the man
Said "Never mind the flavour, who are you?
I could help you with your voice", and through
That man Lloyd was trained in public speaking
By one of the leading speech dramatists in the nation.
Then in a school speaking competition, Lloyd won
Never imagining that next would come
Victory in a national speaking competition,
And a scholarship, in the time of a depression,
To University where in the course of time
He came to know Christ. Then in line
With God's will for him he was soon speaking

To a million people every day on televsion,
Where his programme was called "Let God love you"
(What a healthy, vigorous point of view!).
Lloyd served as a minister in Holywood,
And then came the time when he eventually stood
Opening daily the U.S. Senate in prayer,
Chosen as the spiritual chaplain, there.
With the world's greatest superpower, he was at the core
What a long way from the fridge in that childhood's store!
Ah! Influence! Who can measure its force
As, particularly, teacher's words take their course?
That speech dramatist changed that teenagers's career
By giving to him of his skill and care.
I remember, once staying at the beautiful Faison mansion,
And Mollie Faison had known an incredible conversion
To Jesus Christ, there in Charlotte, North Carolina
And of that Southern hospitality there is nothing finer.
While there I made a radio documentary at that time
For the BBC. The task became mine
Of covering a Billy Graham Crusade
In Charlotte, and three hundred thousand people made
Their way to those services. I remember listening
To Dr. Graham tell a story truly fascinating:
He spoke of the first morning after he'd been converted,
When his schoolteacher from normality averted.
She said to her class with a sarcastic tongue's curl
"I hear we've got a preacher with us this mornin'" and a girl
That Billy liked gave him a withering look,
Such that his very constitution shook.
That statement was still hurting that preacher
Though it was now exactly sixty two years later!
And suddenly I thought that night,
This service will later be broadcast right
Across the United States and will be seen
By millions on their television screens.
Would that teacher ever have dreamt

That those few sarcastic words would one day be sent
From the mouth of that farmboy, then sixteen, in her class
Across her nation after sixty two years had passed?
Of course the fact that stands out at this story's core
Is that those few words are what she is remembered for!
And who of us haven't ever said
Things that now fill us with dread?
If it were not for the forgiveness of the Lord,
We would all have fallen under judgement's sword.
Meanwhile, at home through those years it was pleasant
To have as an anchor at "Tuesday night at the Crescent"
The help of a gifted husband and wife team,
Whose commitment was dedicated and keen
As they played organ and piano hundreds of times, together
With those huge congregations; and never, ever
Can I thank them enough for the help they gave,
As the singing soared wave upon wave ~
Ivor Jones, a superb organist who is a stickler
For insisting that music be followed in every particular.
My roving innovations with singing he used to reel in
Which was not an easy task for him!
Hilary, his wife, followed his classical tradition,
And kept the standard high and on the admission
Of the Godly Jim Whitley who put it very well,
As across the years we heard those voices swell:
In worship of God across the years,
In the midst of all our heartaches and fears,
He said if he had a clear choice
He'd have loved to have gone to Heaven in full voice
Directly from an evening of Tuesday night praise,
As we all had to God our voices raised!
Others helped us with enthusiasm and flair
When Ivor and Hilary were not able to be there
And high praise is also distinctly due
To my good friend Sydney Jeffers who
Came each Tuesday night from Portadown,

And for playing his euphonium he was renowned.
Sydney's kindly words and love for the Saviour
Added a distinctly spiritual flavour
To our lives together as a team
Helped and supported by his wife Irene.
Year after year a friend researched material for me,
And behind the scenes he proved to be,
A deeply valued part of the work of the Lord
In helping me teach the word of God.
Andrew Davis became as my right arm
And to him I thankfully affirm,
That if even a cup of cold water brings its reward
He's in for huge blessing from the Lord!
And Noel McCormick, who stood, week by week,
With me on the door and with handshake would greet
The tide of humanity who came along
To attend the teaching and to join in the song,
Deserves a medal for his cheerful spirit,
Much praise he distinctly merits.
I'm so grateful to the people who met to pray with me,
People like Alan and Carl and Anne Coffey,
Who before each Tuesday service were seen
Gathering with the indominable Mrs. Green.
One night when trouble was in the city,
She did not lean upon any self pity;
Though no buses were running she came out and walked
Several miles to the service, and as we talked
She said, "I'm not going to let the IRA stop me
Hearing the Word of God." I could see
That such people were the salt of the earth.
And as for the purposes of God I searched,
In life and history I could see clearly displayed
His grace in the lives of such people, who were not afraid
To live for Christ no matter what their circumstance,
As the Kingdom of God in the nineties advanced.

I was walking one evening at twilight,
When an awesome woman came into my sight.
She is diminutive in height but not in greatness.
She is a Jewish Auschwitz survivor and her nearness

Of all the world's a coffee shop,
Mr. Fantastic and the Auschwitz survivor

Raising children is a learning curve
(Ours were raised on Calpol, with verve!).
It was a superb medicine to bring temperatures down
And there was always a bottle of it, around.
If one observed the twins in childhood one saw,
They usually had a pen or pencil and they would draw
All kinds of objects, and it was clear from the start
That they had a definite leaning towards Art.
I always claim that God sent Claire to cheer us up,
And her sense of humour would constantly erupt
Into hilarious situations which lit up our day,
And that humour still bubbles, I'm glad to say.
Her understanding and passionate care
For the disadvantaged is real, and there
Is a unique and inspiring trait to her art
Which reaches the page from deep in her heart.
Kerrie is also observant and gifted, and I don't surmise
In saying she has a deep capacity to empathise.
If she believes in something, she is wholehearted,
And from her twin she will seldom be parted.

I will always treasure something Kerrie said
When faced with a statement an unbelieving journalist made.
He had a problem with God in his mind
Because he felt it was strange to find
That God wanted everyone to worship Him ~
He thought it egotistical, almost accusing God of sin.
I asked Kerrie what she thought of what he'd outlined:
"He's looking at it from an earthly perspective", she replied.
It was just lovely to hear such spiritual truth
From Kerrie in the prime of her youth,
And indeed God, whose thoughts are not our thoughts, for sure,
Is a sinless God who will forever endure.
All through Taughmonagh Primary School and Victoria College
The delightful result of much of the knowledge
The twins gained was the desire to communicate visually
What they each knew individually.
Presently as students at the University of Ulster
Their studies have helped to carefully foster
Their gift, and, with focus and care,
Their work flourishes with enthusiastic flair.
The love we feel for our children is beyond words on a page;
The Bible says that such are the Lord's heritage.
Recently we had some children up to our home
From the Ormeau Road area of our city, and one
Of those children cornered me with a look
And fired me a question which brought me "to book":
"Which one do you like best?" she asked of my children ,
And I can honestly say to her and any who question
That I love each one equally but in a different way,
For each one has been unique from the very first day.
Kathryn, whose desire was always to teach,
With huge commitment and focus reached
Her goal and when Victoria College gave her a prize
Called the "Bel Espirit", we were not surprised.
And from Chancellor Julia Neuberger's hand we could see
Kathryn receive a first class honours degree.

Then came a very courteous young man in an MG
And soon it was plain for all to see
That they were in love and an engagement ring shone
To say that a wedding day would soon be along,
And, on the twenty third of December
We, with real and undiluted pleasure,
Watched Kathryn marry David Livingstone
On a day of joy laced with lots of fun.
To see our children follow the Lord
Is a privilege that no earthly reward
Could match, and for their tomorrows
We wish them the Lord's touch, which adds no sorrow.
To all who have helped them we would give deep thanks ,
Particularily to Marjorie Shawcross, who came in the first rank!
And to Bobby and Betty Jordan who deep kindness have shown,
For they treated them as if they were their very own!
Through many days of raising our children,
When at school or College we had left them,
We would slip in through a green door
And, for half an hour or more,
We'd have a scone or crepe the Manus way
To help begin the pattern of the day.
Manus McConn was up with the morning sun
And he made "Randal's" his Coffee Shop, a lot of fun.
His scones were delicious, his crepes something else
And although across Belfast feelings were tense,
Inside "Randal's" around a coffee cup
People a real Community spirit began to sup.
They were drawn from all over Northern Ireland society,
People whose opinions displayed lots of variety.
Let me try to catch the spirit of the place,
As my memory a typical morning would trace:
I mean, take this corner where Roger sits,
Reading "The Independent" between coffee sips;
Or here is Jim McMullan, a member of the police,
A "Daily Telegraph" scans between his eats;

Or there's "Curly" Raymond reading his "Today",
"Morning all", he laughingly will say ;
There bends Bridie, over her "Irish News",
A crossword she solves but a cross word does not use;
And there's Andy Graham reading the "Dunoon Advertiser" ~
Of his local Scottish roots he is now much the wiser;
The people actually sat on pews, that's what they were ,
Bought by Manus with particular care.
If those pews could have talked of who had sat
Upon them, it would make a story that
Would be better than many a story of fiction,
As people came from every direction.
The London "Times" man would come and the man from Sky News
And ITN's Tom Bradby, who gave millions his views;
And there is the island's editor for the "Daily Mail " ~
All had a scone and later they would assail
The difficult task of trying to explain,
What was going on in Ulster time and again.
A society divided with sectarian fracture,
But "Randal's" happily gave them a balanced picture.
Now, who is that flash of lightening coming through the door?
It's Joe Costley coming back for more;
And who is his shadow who is always cheery?
It's Peter Love coming in from County Londonderry;
At half-past nine in slips "The Mouse" ~
Pat is the quietest lady in the house.
She pours Andrew Murphy's third coffee and sweeps the mats
And wears those smashing floppy hats.
Tall, dark and handsome sits the friendly Karen,
To "Randal's" she certainly is not foreign,
And with her friend Loretto, she is never terse:
Here they often overhaul the Universe!
Now what shall we say of the fair Sinead
Whose laughing voice comes to our aid?
Or Nuala and Jackie, now there's a twist ~
We think them twins or was there something we missed?

The Rector's wife finds it a cinch
To slip in to "Randal's" from Ballynahinch ;
And Mrs. Kerr gives us all a smile,
And stays to chat with us awhile.
All these people and more much pleasure found
With Johnston's coffee only served around .
Here troubles and worries and maybe many a scandal
People tried to leave outside of the door of "Randal's".
Manus married Jane one Boxing Day,
And all of us would have to say
That whereas Jane gained a devoted husband,
Manus married the image of Barbara Striesand!
Years before I had bought my Belfast house
From one of the greatest characters about:
Stanley Reid ran a shoe business on Sandy Row
And tens of thousands of people would go
To "Reids" for a definite, useful bargain.
Stanley was a man who pushed the margin
Of life as far as he reasonably could,
For even in the Himalaya's he stood
Or high on many a Scottish moor,
Or deep in a bluebell wood in Oxfordshire.
He loved the outdoors and with his friends
He walked the West Highland Way from end to end
He travelled far and wide, and, he brimmed with laughter
And with us all, forever after,
He left a word of what he thought of life
In all its burgeoning and he was right:
"Fantastic!" Stanley would constantly say
Of the conflagration of sights that came his way.
He was enchanted by the loveliness of nature:
"Fantastic!" he'd say of star or creature.
"I mean, it stands to reason" he'd comment as he'd foray
Into some detail of Nature's outstanding glory,
And then he'd link what he saw with the Creator.
His was a reasonable faith, and later

The word "Fantastic" would again appear ~
It was a word that was always near,
To cover even that which he did not understand
But which intriqued him: what a man!
And he played at hundreds of services on his accordion,
With his good friend Wilbert Henderson,
And with Rosemary his wife, so gifted with creativity
They raised their family with great ability.
With Stanley's death, a light went out
From our lives, and as in my mind I go about
Looking at many of the people and events I've been privilged to know
"Fantastic!" is a word for which I'd go.
Yet life, though fantastic, is constantly threatened
By evil, which has many a subtle weapon.
One is prejudice, which my friend Alex Easton said
"Is the greatest enemy of truth", and it has made
Incalculable rivers of blood to gruesomely flow
Whenever it is allowed, unchecked, to grow.
I was walking one evening at twilight,
When an awesome woman came into my sight.
She is diminutive in height but not in greatness.
She is a Jewish Auschwitz survivor and her nearness
To me that night on the Lisburn Road
Triggered a question which I sought to unload.
Dr. Helen Lewis endured a horrendous fate
And passed Dr. Mengele's table twice and escaped
The gas chamber, and the escaping Nazis took her with them
As the encircling Russians slowly closed in.
Helen fell into a snowdrift and the guards did not see
Her crawl away upon her knees.
She later came to Northern Ireland at the end of the war
And many of our troubles she had to endure.
She loved it here despite its dark side
And she has been an inspiration far and wide.
Her writing is honed powerfully and well

In her memoirs entitled "A time to tell".
"Helen", I said, as I stopped for a chat,
"What is your hope for a new Millenium?" and at that,
She turned to me as quick as a flash:
"Tolerance", she said without batting an eyelash.
"And tolerance will lead to understanding", she explained,
And then with a wistful smile, as a new breath she gained.
She said words which still ring in my ear
And which I wish millions of people could hear:
"And understanding might even lead to affection", she said
And often I think of the statement she made
As the Jewish Holocaust recedes into history.
It still remains to me a mystery
How people can kill others for their religious views
In human life it is daily news.
"Put your sword back in its place", Jesus said
To Peter when his sword he thrust
At the High Priest's servant called Malchus
In the Garden of Gethsemane; and Christ's view
Was clearly given to the Roman Governor, Pilate
Before whom he was not silent:
"My kingdom is not of this world", he declared,
"If it were then my servants would fight", and he inferred
That any use of force to further His cause
Was strictly forbidden because
His kingdom is based on love, not force.
When I think of Nazi hatred taking its fearful course,
Or sectarian hatred on numerous occasions,
Killing people of a different persuasion,
I know if the final judgement of God towards it were slack,
Heaven would certainly turn black.
But the judge of all the earth will do right
In all judgement brought before his sight.
Yet, may understanding grow in the land of my birth,
And of affection may there be no dearth,

And may the killing stop and peaceable living reign
And blood from violence never flow again.
May this beautiful place of valley and hill
Be transformed by God's help and a people's will.

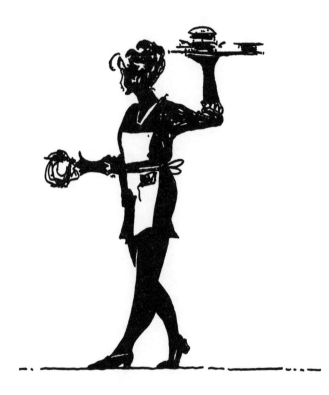

I was in an East Belfast restaurant called the "Red Rooster"
And I remember clearly seeing her
Approach my family at the table
To serve us, as she was able.
Suddenly something from her heart came out
Which sums up what my life has been all about.
She said, "I was at your Bible Class last night"

Of the lady at the "Red Rooster" and one final question

The last centimetre of chalk separating England and France
Had fallen away as the Channel Tunnel advanced;
And Yelstin now ruled Russia and John Major tried
To unite the divided Tories and terrorists defied.
Mary Robinson became the first woman ever
To become President of the Republic of Ireland, and never
Had a woman in six centuries been elected
As Speaker of the House of Commons and Betty Boothroyd was selected;
And Janet Reno became the Attorney General of the United States,
Power was opening up to women its long shut gates;
And Kim Campbell, in her agenda,
Became the first woman Prime Minister of Canada;
And Toni Morrison became the first African-American woman
To win Literature's Nobel prize; and summoned
To be first woman justice on Japan's Supreme Court
Was Hisako Takahashi; and, of course
The inspiring Aung San Sun Kyi, the Burmese Opposition leader,
Won the Nobel Peace prize and later
Talked from her gate to the whole world
While enduring a house arrest which continues to be just absurd.

The Hubble Space Telescope kept probing
The far reaches of space, discovering
Galaxies we never knew exsisted,
Billions of stars we had never listed.
Apartheid was abolished in legislation
In South Africa and long standing bitter relations
Were breached by Mandela and De Klerk;
And the Internet and The Web helped the search
For information beyond what we had dreamed
And both of them now have seemed
To bring the concept of Cyberspace close to reality
And life will never return to its former normality.
In America Bill Clinton defeated President George Bush,
And the years for me now began to rush.
I had Bible Classes in Glasgow, Edinburgh and Belfast,
And precious seed I continued to cast.
The third class was in Palmertson Place in "Auld Reekie"
And in fellowship with Neill Innes and his committee
I again saw the surfacing proof
Of the power of taught Scripture which is not aloof
From being relevant to passing history ~
Its message is a wonderful revealing mystery.
I also visited the Dominion of Canada in line
With a deeply held principle of mine:
"Act local, think global" is a good principle to follow,
And in Vancouver, St. Catherine's and Toronto
I taught God's Word and also tried to constantly write
Books in which it was a privilege to exalt Christ.
From a little book on Ruth written when I was twenty four,
I have now been privileged to write nineteen more ,
And a lot of them were typed by my dedicated friend, Jean Clent,
Who worked so hard and to me was sent,
To help with much secretarial work,
And from pressure she certainly did not shirk.
Deidre Cousins too typed up books with care
Always working with a cheerful air,

And if only one line of those books has helped to inspire
Someone, somewhere facing something dire,
Life has been worth living, believe me.
One of those books was a biography
Of Dr. TBF Thompson, the industrialist,
Who for the cause of Christ is an enthusiast.
This has led, with him, to a fresh ministry of Christian literature
Which brings me the very deepest pleasure
As we try to present stories of the Christian faith
And in strategic places to have them placed.
Weekly in the "Fraserburgh Herald" I also wrote ,
Published in the fishing community of Scotland's North East Coast.
I also wrote a weekly column for the "Belfast Telegraph" newspaper
And it led to a fascinating interview with the Duke of Westminster,
One of the most impressive public figures I have ever met.
He is a man deeply dedicated to family values, and yet,
Despite his great wealth I found him deeply humble
And helping thousands of people in all kinds of trouble.
I asked him "What would be a luxury to you?"
He intimated that this question to him was not new
Such a question irritated him, he said
For in his charity work he was often led
To see distressing things and, he added emphatically,
"Four healthy children are a luxury".
How right His Grace is, for money could never buy
Such a luxury for any family.
Now, though, as my life faced a new decade
And as a new Millenium began to pervade
On the horizon of all our lives,
God slowly but surely began to confide
With me by various signs
That now was the appointed time
For me to move on in His plan for my future;
And in the decision I found great nurture
From the story of the Bible's Philip, who when God called him on
And from Samaria towards Gaza, he walked along

He soon learned that it was Ethiopia God had in mind ~
What an incredible thing to find!
And so Margaret and I moved on to ChristChurch, Belfast in
God's service,
Believing that God was distinctly leading us,
And now I serve there as a teaching pastor.
And I also serve as a broadcaster
Weekly with Trans World Radio,
Broadcasting across the nations of Europe, even though
I deserve it not, the Lord has given to me,
The privilege of a fascinating ministry.
Soon, God willing, I shall visit Japan
To teach at their Keswick Convention.
And as my life now turns to new days,
I look back with affection on the ways
The gracious Lord has led me through
Somehow clearly into my view
One incident stands out beyond them all,
And often its details I recall:
I was in an East Belfast restaurant called the "Red Rooster"
And I remember clearly seeing her
Approach my family at the table
To serve us, as she was able.
Suddenly something from her heart came out
Which sums up what my life has been all about.
She said, "I was at your Bible Class last night"
I was surprised for I had not caught sight
Of Jackie in the gathered crowd.
"It's different!", she said, out loud
And then came the line of lines for me,
Summing up clearly what Jacqui could see:
"It's different! It stays with you", she said.
"It must be the Bible", and I'm not afraid
To say that Jacqui gave me the greatest compliment I've ever known
From what the Holy Spirit had shown
To her soul that night as the Word was taught ,

And whose very essence she had caught.
Jacqui died recently of cancer
And when I get to Heaven I will find her
And tell her that those lovely words,
Which in that restaurant simply occurred,
Have blessed me more than I can express ~
I'm so grateful for her kindness.
And, sure, was it not what my mother had taught me
As a teenager about the Bible's Mary?
That she chose that better part with certainty
Which won't be taken from her for all eternity.
I thank God for the grace and help he has given
To reach out with His word which is powerful and living,
And to Him I give all of the glory
For all He has done in my life and in my story.
One recent invitation gives me deep nostalgic pleasure
While I have sought to guage and measure
 My pathway in these lines of verse ~
It was to preach at Cambridge University Christian Union where,
of course
I had been inspired by Dr. Martyn Lloyd-Jones,
And I go there knowing I'm not alone.
For maybe as, with God's help, I do what he sought to do
Some young person listening may seek anew
To give their life to teaching the Word of God.
For this Jacqui I'm sure would applaud,
For after all "It's different" you see,
"It stays with you", she would agree!
When I was born my half-sister Margaret said,
"Frederick" was too big a name for such a small baby and made,
A suggestion that my name be cut in two,
And I be called "Derick", so, I was named anew!
And now as fifty three years I have traced,
I have one last question which I would raise.
I was born in Newry, County Down, as a twin
In Dr. Hagan's Nursing Home, and then

After two days my little brother died,
And this question is now raised in my mind:
What has he been doing all of these years
In that place where God wipes away all tears?